Contents

Part Three: Optional activities for older pupils

Developing Patterns in Physical Education

A. Bilbrough

Diploma, Carnegie College of Physical Education
Formerly Senior Organiser of Physical Education,
Lancashire County Council

Percy Jones

Diploma, Carnegie College of Physical Education
Area Organiser of Physical Education,
Lancashire County Council

 University of London Press Ltd

A/613.7

ISBN 0 340 06590 7 Boards
ISBN 0 340 16791 2 Unibook

University of London Press Ltd
St Paul's House, Warwick Lane, London EC4P 4AH

Printed and bound in England by
Butler & Tanner Ltd, Frome and London

List of figures

Part I

10

Preface

In our book *Physical Education in the Primary School*[1] we set out to give practical help and guidance to teachers on the content and teaching method of a modern approach to physical education in general, and to gymnastics in particular. Though the book was written mainly for non-specialist teachers in infant and junior schools, we are led to believe that it has also proved to be of real value to specialist teachers in secondary schools.

Our long association with physical education at all levels, our involvement in the many changes and developments which have characterised the post-war period, our experience in the practical, administrative and advisory aspects of the work, together with a desire to give further help and guidance to specialist teachers and students in colleges of education, have encouraged us to write this second book. In it, our intention has been to consider the more recent historical, philosophical and developmental aspects of physical education, rather than to deal specifically with teaching technique or subject material. On the other hand, there is a distinctly practical emphasis on the administration and organisation of physical education in secondary schools.

The book is divided into three main parts. Part One deals with the trends and developments of recent years. The term *physical education* is interpreted and assessed, whilst the problems associated with the expanding scope and content of the curriculum are given careful consideration. The basic educational principles which have inspired new methods of teaching in many aspects of physical education are also discussed.

In Part Two, the personal and material factors which influence the planning of a physical education programme are considered. Stages of development in the implementation of a programme are

[1] University of London Press Ltd, 3rd edition 1968.

11

suggested and the illustrative material shows how the use of simple pro formae minimises the practical problems associated with the preparation and recording of schemes of work.

Part Three is concerned with one of the most significant of recent trends in physical education in secondary schools – optional activities for older pupils. Practical solutions are suggested to the many problems encountered when an options programme is embarked upon, for experience has shown that many essential conditions must be satisfied if this important development in physical education is to be successful and rewarding.

We wish to thank the many teachers and headteachers who have given us their help and cooperation at all times and to acknowledge the valuable contribution made by the quotations we have used from numerous articles and publications. These extracts have helped considerably to substantiate our own personal views and ideas.

Finally, we should like to thank our publishers for their kindly assistance and valuable advice throughout the preparation of this book.

A. BILBROUGH
PERCY JONES
January 1973

Part One

Trends and developments in physical education

1 Our changing world

It is probably true to say that developments in physical education
since the end of the Second World War have been the most progressive in the long history of physical education in schools. But is this
really surprising in view of the dramatic changes which have taken
place during this period in almost every aspect of our society and of
the world around us? There have been periods in our history when
little has changed for a long time and progress has been virtually nil.
Certainly, the period since 1945 cannot be regarded in this way.

A 'trend' has been defined as 'a movement in a given direction
towards a point not yet reached', or as 'the path along which ideas
have travelled, are travelling, or will probably travel'. Development
implies progress, the growth of new concepts, ideas, methods and
techniques. It is therefore appropriate, before changes in education
or physical education are discussed, to remind ourselves of the
tremendous progress made in recent years on many fronts – scientific,
economic, domestic, social, technological, medical, commercial, industrial and so on. Computers, space research, jet travel and heart
transplantation have become part of the general conversation of
ordinary people who have become familiar with rapid and frequent
changes in fashion, design, art, industry and commerce. New ideas
are the product of experimentation, exploration and research – taxing
man's intelligence, initiative, inventiveness, imagination, ingenuity,
originality, enterprise and creative ability and challenging his capacity
to think and to apply his knowledge and experience to a variety of
demanding situations.

Reference to these changes and developments is made if only to
remind ourselves that, just as changes take place in other aspects of
our lives, so changes in various aspects of the educational structure
must also be expected and should not be regarded in any way as
surprising.

14

Speaking at a conference on 'The Educational Implications of Social and Economic Change' called by the Schools Council, Professor P. H. Taylor, Professor of Curriculum and Method at the University of Birmingham, said, 'Each profession seeks for a strategy to help it to deal with the many and formidable problems suddenly confronting it. None rejects the problems. A strategy for education must have regard to the nature of the society in which it has its setting and the principles on which that society is based. No strategy is worth its salt unless it communicates confidence.'

Acceptance of change, or certainly a willingness to consider it, is a natural outcome of a progressive outlook and attitude, and there are many aspects of educational change which reflect the progressive attitude of educationists during the last two decades. A survey of the educational scene during this time clearly indicates that it has been a period of unprecedented development, progress and challenge. By some it has been described as an intellectual revolution, and by others a period of new learning, perhaps a second Renaissance. At the Schools Council Conference already referred to, Sir Ronald Gould, formerly General Secretary of the National Union of Teachers, said, 'If there were no economic and social changes, there would be no educational implications. The significant thing about today is not that there are changes, but that there are so many and they rapidly succeed each other. The rapidity of change and the scale of change mark the difference between this and earlier ages. The consequences for the schools are many. The content of education, for example, is changing quite substantially . . . the techniques are different . . . the organisation of schools is altered . . . and changes have also come in the provision of education.' After referring to the re-structuring of infant and junior schools, the development of comprehensive schools, the raising of the school leaving age, the development of nursery schools, the extension to three and sometimes four years of the courses in colleges of education, the rapidly developing and expanding colleges of further education, colleges of technology, and universities, he went on to say, 'So the educational scene today shows that social and economic changes are affecting the content, methods and the shape of the educational system.'

2 Educational changes

Although it is recognised that the era since 1945 has been a period of progress and of new learning, it must also be appreciated that it has been a period of problems, of experimentation, of trial and sometimes of error. Everything has not always proceeded according to plan; everything that has been tried has not always succeeded. In all aspects of education those involved in and concerned with change and new developments have passed through stages of doubt, disappointment and comparative insecurity, but perhaps this in itself is a worthwhile educational experience in which a demand is made upon perseverance and determination in the face of apparent failure or defeat.

Teachers embarking on the implementation of new ideas in the teaching of any subject, academic or practical, often experience a sense of insecurity and there is a temptation to reject new ideas and methods if they are not immediately successful. Fortunately, there have been teachers with determination, understanding, sincerity, conviction and enthusiasm who have resisted this temptation and who have successfully established a modern conception of education, realising that those who make no mistakes make nothing. During this period, probably more than at any other time in educational history, attempts have been made, in the teaching of all subjects, to fit education to the child, rather than the child to education – a familiar phrase, but a challenge to any teacher, of any subject, using any method or approach.

At all levels of education, nursery, primary, secondary, further and higher, considerable improvement has been seen in the scale and standards of provision, not only of more adequate buildings and other facilities but also of equipment and materials. There have also been considerable changes, particularly at school level, in the scope, content and methods employed in the teaching of practically every subject of the curriculum. Teachers have become familiar with new methods of teaching mathematics and science, reading and art, with the use of the initial teaching alphabet, with programmed learning, language laboratories, closed circuit television, the integrated day, open planning and the use of an ever increasing variety of visual and teaching aids. More than at any other time in the development of educational theory and practice this has been the period of the individual when the methods developed and now widely employed allow for greater flexibility and freedom, for less regimentation, mechanical learning and instruction. In all subjects, not least in physical education, successful attempts have been made to accommodate each child individually and, as Dr D. H. Parker, educational psychologist, says in his book *Schooling for Individual Excellence*,[1] 'to provide a schooling structure in which each child may start

[1] Nelson, 1964.

16

where he is and move as fast as his learning rate and capacity will let him'.

'From each according to his ability, to each according to his need' has been the philosophy that has inspired much successful progress in recent years. The aim at all times is to develop to the full the individual talent, ability and capacity of each child.

3 Extremes and the middle way

In both education and physical education this period has seen extreme formality and teacher domination on the one hand, and extreme informality and freedom on the other. During the last few years these extremes have come closer together and although there are differences in the ways in which individual teachers apply current methods, in all subjects they endeavour to satisfy the same basic and fundamental principles which recognise the individuality of each child and which exploit the advantages of both formal and informal teaching.

In this philosophy the best of the old merges with the best of the new to produce what might be termed *the middle way*. Figure 1 illustrates diagrammatically this merging of contrasting ideas, attitudes and techniques. The left hand side of the diagram represents those opinions and teaching methods which are characterised by complete formality, rigidity and teacher domination. The right hand side represents those ideas, methods and techniques which have diametrically opposed characteristics. During the last twenty years both these extremist views have had their ardent and enthusiastic devotees and both have been the subject of unqualified support on the one hand and severe criticism on the other. As the undoubted values of both concepts have become more clearly apparent and appreciated by extremists at both ends of the scale, a slow but gradual modification of the practical application of the principles involved has become apparent. There has been an acknowledgment and acceptance by each of the other's point of view and to a greater or lesser degree the extremists have incorporated into the teaching methods used some of the features and techniques of one another's philosophy. Thus, as the diagram suggests, the formal becomes less formal and the informal less informal – both gradual processes – until each individual teacher finds the mixture of the old and the new which best suits him. While the majority of teachers, in due course, will reach the middle way where formal and informal, direct and

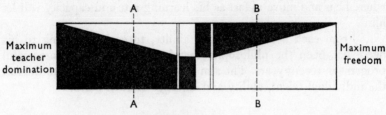

FIGURE I   *Extremes and the middle way*

Old fashioned education		New–fashioned education
Class methods of instruction		Individual methods of teaching
Formality		Informality
Teacher–imposed methods		Child–centred methods
Direct teaching		Indirect teaching
'Do it this way'–teacher directed		'Do it your way!' – self directed
Training		Educating
Skill learning		Skill using
The process of 'putting in'		The process of 'bringing out'
Regimentation and rigidity		Freedom and flexibility
Everything must be taught.		The child discovers everything
Rote learning and mechanical instruction		Children placed in problem solving situations
Little opportunity for exploration		Maximum opportunity for experimentation
Minimum opportunity for individual choice		Maximum opportunity for individual choice
Traditional methods produce high standards		Traditional methods limit progress
Resistance to new ideas		Total acceptance of new ideas
Retain the best of the old	AND	Adopt the best of the new

FIGURE 2   *The middle way*

indirect, traditional and modern methods are balanced and equally intermingled, it must be accepted that others will operate somewhere between points A and B, depending upon their personal inclination towards and sympathies with the old or the new. The individuality of teachers must be recognised and variations of approach expected.

18

Figure 2 illustrates the opposing and often conflicting ideas, attitudes and methods which, by moving towards each other, produce a sensible and extremely successful middle way, a current trend of immense significance in the fields of education and physical education.

A. N. Whitehead in his book *The Aims of Education*[1] undoubtedly shares this view. He says: 'The real point is to discover in practice that exact balance between freedom and discipline which will give the greatest range of progress over the things to be known.'

4 Age, aptitude and ability

Since the end of the Second World War, teachers have endeavoured to fulfil the requirements of the 1944 Education Act – to educate children according to age, aptitude and ability. Which of these considerations is of the greatest importance? Perhaps the answer is found in the words of Elizabeth Fry, who said: 'Children should be educated according to aptitude and ability rather than age.'

In all aspects of education there is ample evidence to support the view that the chronological factor is not the most important and that frequently the abilities and aptitudes of some children far exceed those of an older age group. This is perhaps especially true in physical education where so many younger children display outstanding natural ability and confidence. These are exhibited particularly in gymnastics, swimming, games and all aspects of physical activity and lead to the conclusion that Elizabeth Fry's view can be substantiated and that any teaching method used must be based on the aim of exploiting to the full the individual ability and aptitude of each child, a challenge which teachers now readily accept.

5 Training and education

The period under review has been one in which the essential differences between training and education have been more fully appreciated. Dr D. H. Parker, in *Schooling for Individual Excellence*, says:

'Animals can be trained, they cannot be educated. Only man can be educated, but man must first be trained in order to be

[1] Benn, 1932.

A/613.7   19

educated. He must first get the skills needed to generate knowledge. Skill getting is training, it is not education. Next man must learn how to use these skills to generate knowledge and put it to use to fulfil his needs. Skill using is education . . . Education is concerned with something far beyond the mere reflex-like acquisition and performance of a skill, it is concerned with the decision-making process. The main business of education is to help the individual learn how to gather data, form hypotheses, test hypotheses and draw conclusions as a guide to intelligent action. Education is concerned with the whats, whys, whens, wheres and hows of a situation in which skill is used.'

Dr Parker continues:

'We have seen how training and education are different from each other. It is easy to see that separate times must be provided during the school day for each. Yet how can we blend them together so that a pupil does not come up with simply a bundle of skills and not enough knowledge or experience in applying them, to live intelligently? Can both training and education live compatibly side by side in the same class-room? I think they can. The secret is this – the two must be continually blended.'

Surely this is what those engaged in the teaching of physical education have attempted to achieve in recent years and Dr Parker's philosophy, as well as his practical suggestions for implementing his ideas, can be directly applied to current theory and practice in physical education. Teachers have endeavoured to equip their pupils with the skill and ability to use their bodies confidently and effectively in a wide variety of different situations. On the hills, on or in the water, on the playing field or in the gymnasium, children are placed in problem-solving, decision-making situations which allow them opportunities, individually, to draw conclusions and then to take intelligent and appropriate action. The important factor is that the children are given opportunities to increase their personal skill and to find their own solutions to the many physical problems with which they are faced. Frequent opportunities are provided for experimentation and exploration and for the educational experiences of skill-using, of decision-making and of taking intelligent action. As Dr Parker says: 'Education is concerned on the one hand with the mastery of skills and on the other with the development of powers of expression and imagination and the intelligent application of skill. Education suffers if either is neglected – they are complementary.'

20

6 Physical education – an interpretation

It is not our intention to outline in detail the story of the introduction of physical education into the school curriculum, nor to deal with the factors which have influenced its progress over many years, because these aspects have been discussed adequately and comprehensively in many excellent publications dealing specifically with the history of physical education. An important development, however, has been the general acceptance of the term physical education as distinct from physical training.

The Board of Education's *Syllabus of Physical Training for Schools* (1933) clearly indicated the intended interpretation of the scope of physical education in schools, when it stated: 'Physical Education includes all activities likely to minister to physical health, not only gymnastics, games, swimming and dancing, but sports, free play, walking tours, school journeys, camps and all forms of occupation and exercise likely to create a love of the open air and a healthy way of living. Physical Training given at, or in connection with the school, is only a part, though a very important part of the whole subject.'

This is the interpretation of physical education which is held by many today, but if the term is to be used with complete justification, surely it must imply something more than merely a change of terminology. It should mean something more than drill and training. What does it mean?

The term physical education appears to have been given two interpretations. As already suggested in the 1933 syllabus, it is used to indicate the umbrella under which all aspects of physical activity are embraced. It implies an ever-widening range of activities such as games, gymnastics, athletics, swimming, sailing, canoeing, and so on, which combine to produce a comprehensive programme. Alternatively, the term is often used when referring to the indoor lesson which was previously known as drill, physical training, or gymnastics. We then have the games, the athletics or the swimming lesson on the one hand, and the P.E. lesson on the other. Is this latter interpretation a confusing and too limited a conception of what is really meant? Are games, dance, athletics, swimming, and so on not a part of physical education?

To fulfil the requirements and aims of education in its broadest sense, children must be given something which has a lasting and beneficial effect, something which leaves on each individual child a

21

permanent impression which will affect thought, action and behaviour throughout life. It is a combination of the effect on the pupil of the teacher, the subject and the methods used. This applies to the teaching of all subjects and physical education is no exception. An appreciation of physical fitness, a desire for a healthy way of living, a keenness for high standards of hygiene, an acceptance of moral values in terms of fair play, of modesty in victory and generosity in defeat, the development of physical ability, regular participation in healthy physical activity, the contribution to leisure-time pursuits, the capacity to develop and use initiative, a ready willingness to accept responsibility and the capacity to cooperate with others are all factors which contribute to the education of the individual. They all have their own particular educational value, but it is in their total impact that the educational effect is of permanent and lasting benefit and many of these factors are the special and particular responsibility of physical education.

Though there may be other requirements, to be fully educational in the particular sense, there must be an exploratory and an inventive element present in the teaching methods used and the work must be based on the realisation of the individuality of each member of the class or group. A thought process must be involved and understanding must accompany performance. In the light of these requirements can it be claimed with complete confidence and conviction that the more traditional methods used when teaching many aspects of physical activity were, in fact, educational? We would never doubt the educational values to be derived when a subject is presented by a gifted teacher whose relationship with the children, example and standards are of the highest quality. There are, however, some teachers in the field of physical education who continue to operate on traditional and rigid lines but have re-named their lessons physical education in order to conform to the modern idiom. This is merely paying lip-service to a new terminology.

The educational principles previously outlined are being applied more and more to all aspects of the physical education programme in schools. The presentation of any physical activity in the school situation should be assessed by two criteria, the physical and the educational. The two must go hand-in-hand and neither should suffer by over-emphasis on one. The aims should be:

a   to contribute to the general education of the individual through physical activity;

b   to educate individuals physically, by developing their physical ability, adaptability and versatility in as wide and all-embracing a way as possible;

c   to present physical activities in ways which are based on sound educational principles, so that

i) the individual is faced with situations in which he must exercise a thought process and make those decisions which enable his personal skill to be used to the best advantage in solving the problems set or imposed;

ii) an individual response becomes possible and it is accepted that such individual responses will probably be different;

iii) situations are presented which allow opportunities for the development of initiative, enterprise and creative thinking;

iv) understanding and awareness of the many factors which influence both ideas and performance can be developed.

Games, dance, swimming, athletics, and so on are now being taught with these principles in mind and they can all quite rightly claim to be of educational value and to be regarded as physical education.

We must therefore conclude that the term physical education should refer to the all-embracing and comprehensive programme of physical activities included in a school's syllabus and that each specific aspect should be specifically named. When the drill, or P.T., or P.E. lesson has been so modified and developed that the educational requirements already briefly outlined have been satisfied it is appropriate to refer to the lesson as educational gymnastics and to regard it as a valuable and indeed an essential aspect of a comprehensive physical education programme.

7   The physical education programme

An important trend of the post-war period has been the great expansion in the scope and content of the physical education programme itself. Many teachers will remember, from their own experience at school and from their college training, that physical education included gymnastics, major games, athletics and swimming. The programme rarely included more than these particular aspects and, at school level, frequently less. It can therefore be said with truth that one of the outstanding developments of recent years has been the extension of the scope and width of the physical education programme. (See Fig. 3, page 24.)

Athletics now includes all the usual track and field events and cross-country running; in addition, weight training, circuit training and interval training have become regular features of a training

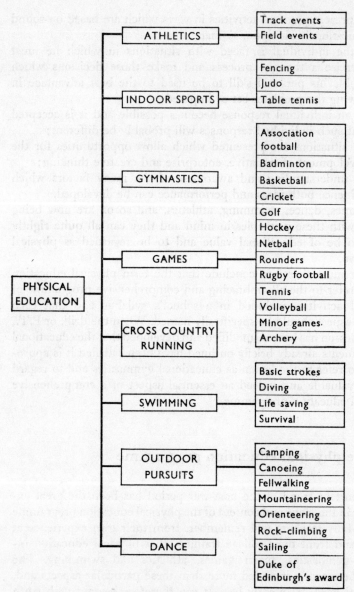

```
                                          ┌─ Track events
                      ┌─ ATHLETICS ────────┤
                      │                     └─ Field events
                      │
                      │                     ┌─ Fencing
                      │                     ├─ Judo
                      ├─ INDOOR SPORTS ─────┤
                      │                     └─ Table tennis
                      │
                      │                     ┌─ Association
                      │                     │   football
                      │                     ├─ Badminton
                      ├─ GYMNASTICS         ├─ Basketball
                      │                     ├─ Cricket
                      │                     ├─ Golf
                      │                     ├─ Hockey
                      │                     ├─ Netball
                      ├─ GAMES ─────────────┼─ Rounders
  PHYSICAL            │                     ├─ Rugby football
  EDUCATION ──────────┤                     ├─ Tennis
                      │                     ├─ Volleyball
                      │                     ├─ Minor games.
                      ├─ CROSS COUNTRY      └─ Archery
                      │   RUNNING
                      │                     ┌─ Basic strokes
                      │                     ├─ Diving
                      ├─ SWIMMING ──────────┤
                      │                     ├─ Life saving
                      │                     └─ Survival
                      │
                      │                     ┌─ Camping
                      ├─ OUTDOOR            ├─ Canoeing
                      │   PURSUITS          ├─ Fellwalking
                      │                     ├─ Mountaineering
                      │                     ├─ Orienteering
                      │                     ├─ Rock–climbing
                      └─ DANCE              ├─ Sailing
                                            └─ Duke of
                                                Edinburgh's award
```

FIGURE 3   *Physical education today*

schedule. Few schools now restrict their major games programme to one summer and one winter game and we find experience of a wider variety of both indoor and outdoor games being available, including badminton, basketball, volleyball, netball, association and rugby football, tennis, hockey, cricket, golf, rounders, stoolball, and a wide variety of minor games and major games practices. Swimming not only includes the teaching of basic swimming strokes and diving techniques but also life-saving, survival swimming and sub-aqua activities. Indoor sports which also find a place in the programme are fencing, trampolining, judo and table-tennis. The introduction of creative dance into the curriculum of both primary and secondary schools has been another significant development in recent years, adding a new dimension to the physical education programme.

Another major trend of the last few years has been the tremendous developments in outdoor pursuits which include such activities as camping, canoeing, sailing, rock-climbing, fell-walking, skiing, orienteering, and mountaineering.

This widening or expansion of the curriculum, while praiseworthy in itself, brings with it many accompanying problems which are related to the need for careful selection and discrimination in planning the programme for a school. These problems will be discussed in detail in Part Two of this book.

Figure 3 indicates the tremendous width of the physical education programme in schools today.

8 Optional activities for older pupils

Another interesting and exciting recent development has been the introduction of optional activities for older pupils. This is an extension of the basic principle that the presentation of opportunities for the exercise of individual choice is educationally sound. It must be recognised, however, that immediately the principle of introducing optional activities is accepted, the planning and implementation of a successful scheme presents particular problems. Satisfactory answers to many questions must be found, for example:

When should options be introduced?
How should this final stage of the programme be organised?
What particular conditions must be satisfied?
What activities can satisfactorily be made available?
How will the scheme be administered?
What limits must be set?
How can staffing problems be solved?
What safety factors must be considered?
What are the financial implications?
How can adequate supplies of equipment be provided?
Careful thought and consideration of these and many other factors

will be required and much research and experimentation will be necessary by those teachers embarking on an options scheme if worthwhile and desirable results are to be achieved. Joint consultation and discussion by teachers from different schools who are planning or conducting schemes, of the problems met and their possible solutions, would be of great value. The practice of allowing individual pupils to exercise personal choice in this way is a relatively recent development which will, without doubt, be a permanent trend of the future.

Guidance and help in planning optional activities for older pupils will be given in Part Three of this book.

9 Outdoor pursuits

Many schools include instruction and practice in a number of outdoor pursuits, not only during school holidays and at weekends but also during school hours, especially during periods when optional activities for older pupils are organised. Most education authorities conduct courses of instruction in these activities for teachers and leaders and many have established their own specially staffed and equipped residential centres where children and teachers enjoy opportunities for experience and training in various outdoor pursuits. These centres are situated in some of the most attractive districts of the British Isles – in the Lake District, North Wales, the Highlands of Scotland, the West Country, and other delightful parts of the coastline and rural areas. Most of these centres were formerly large private residences which have been converted to their present use and provide ideal facilities, not only for the practice of the activities themselves, but also for the valuable social and educational experiences which living in a residential situation permits.

This development of outdoor pursuits has great educational value in addition to the physical demands which are inherent not only in the activities, but also in the natural environment in which they take place. The concentration on opportunities for individual and small group participation in an informal atmosphere, very different from that of the traditional major team games, provides a most valuable educational experience. In addition to the pleasure which is derived from participation in these healthy, demanding and often exciting physical activities, the need to display and to develop qualities of self-reliance, determination, perseverance, concentration, reliability and cooperation, the need for physical fitness and

26

powers of endurance, together with the need to develop the ability to assess a situation and to make sensible personal decisions, make these pursuits particularly valuable character-forming influences. Because these pursuits are mostly of an individual nature or can be easily organised by small groups, and because the personal equipment required is within the range of most pockets, many of these activities have great carry-over value into post-school life. They frequently become absorbing hobbies.

Many publications deal in great detail with the techniques of these pursuits, with equipment and clothing required and with safety precautions to be observed. There is also ample evidence to substantiate the claims made for their physical and educational value. It is therefore not necessary to do more here than to recognise that the recent developments in outdoor pursuits have been amongst the most exciting and valuable of the post-war period.

Great impetus to these developments has been given by the Central Council of Physical Recreation which, with its specially qualified staff and excellently equipped centres, has done much to inspire interest and enthusiasm. Its many recreational courses in sailing, climbing and all types of outdoor pursuits have provided opportunities for many to enjoy and benefit from these activities. Sincere tribute must also be paid to the excellence of the numerous training courses which have been instrumental in equipping so many expert leaders and teachers with the necessary technical knowledge and experience for this work. This contribution has been of incalculable benefit in the development of outdoor pursuits in schools.

The activities associated with the Duke of Edinburgh's Award Scheme have found their way into the curriculum. This scheme has stimulated great interest and activity amongst both boys and girls and has stressed such important features as adventure, fitness, hobbies and service to the community during the important years of adolescence.

10 The provision of facilities

Another important post-war trend which has greatly influenced the development of physical education in all its aspects has been the increased provision of greatly improved facilities and a much more generous supply of apparatus and equipment. An indoor space for physical activity has been recognised as an essential feature of all schools – infant, junior and secondary – so that programmes can be planned which will cater for regular participation in dance, gymnastics, indoor games and games practices. The primary school hall is, in essence, a primary school gymnasium with an extensive range of small equipment and large portable and fixed apparatus such as climbing ropes, scrambling nets, window ladder units, climbing frames and parallel ropes, vaulting boxes, balancing bars and benches, vaulting and agility platforms and large rubber mats. This type of provision is standard in new schools, and many older schools have been modified and equipped in this way. This has been made possible in many instances by school reorganisation. When all-age-range schools have become primary schools and the older children have been transferred to new secondary schools, the hall has become available for physical education purposes.

The revolution which has taken place in the teaching of gymnastics in the primary school, dealt with in our previous book *Physical Education in the Primary School*, has been accompanied by a further significant development in the introduction of swimming instruction as an integral part of the junior school curriculum. In the planning of their swimming schemes, many local education authorities give the highest priority for instruction to junior school children. This has resulted in much greater use of public swimming baths by school classes and has highlighted the need for increased provision of facilities suitable for teaching classes of younger children. The learner pool has been designed to fulfil this purpose and the most usual type has water of a uniform depth of approximately three feet. Many education authorities have provided facilities of this kind and many other learner pools have been provided by parent–teacher associations often in cooperation with the local education authority.

At one time the provision of a playing field was felt only to be essential in schools catering for children over the age of eleven years, but it is now accepted that a playing field is equally essential for primary school children. Such playing fields provide small-size pitches with scaled-down goal posts for major games and spaces suitable for play and practice in small teams or groups. The hard playground area continues to provide a valuable teaching space, especially when suitably marked for games and games practices. These areas become much more valuable if there is a suitable wall surface available for ball practices as they have always provided popular and worthwhile playing areas for practice with either small or large balls, with or without a bat or racquet, and for either individual, partner or group participation.

At the secondary stage, the immediate post-war period was characterised by the provision of a fully-equipped gymnasium in each new secondary school, in addition to playing fields and hard surface playing areas. The more recent trend towards larger schools has made it possible to increase the range of facilities so that schools, according to their size, might now have not only a gymnasium but also a sports hall and a swimming bath, and not only grass pitches for major team games but also artificial cricket wickets, tennis courts, a porous all-weather pitch and either an athletics track or an athletics training area.

The pre-war 60 feet by 30 feet gymnasium has been replaced by an area of approximately 2,800 square feet and because of changing methods in the teaching of gymnastics the range of equipment provided has been increased to provide a greater variety of apparatus situations, which allow better opportunities for experimentation and the development of individual ideas. Previously, schedules for the provision of fixed equipment for gymnastics usually included wall bars along both long sides of the gymnasium, four sets of climbing ropes, four sets of double beams and a vertical window ladder unit. It is now more usual to provide only two sets of climbing ropes and two sets of beams together with the window ladder, but in addition to provide one or two sets of hinged wall bars, several rope ladders, a trapeze, two sets of rings, a horizontal heaving bar and an oblique climbing rope. If sited carefully, this equipment can readily supply the many and varied apparatus situations referred to above. In addition to the balancing benches and the traditional vaulting apparatus – box, horse and buck – most authorities usually provide bar-boxes, vaulting platforms of varying heights, trampettes and trampolines, while the coir-fibre landing mats have been largely replaced by different types of resilient rubber mats. These changes have accompanied developments in teaching methods which have encouraged the use of several types of equipment in combination.

11 Sports halls[1]

Another significant development of the last few years has been the provision for secondary schools of sports halls which provide a much

[1] *Imperial and metric measurements* – It will be noted that imperial measurements are used in this and subsequent sections when reference is made to dimensions of buildings, structural specifications, spacing of games courts, etc. It is appreciated that these measurements will ultimately be replaced by metric alternatives or equivalents. Where metric alternatives or equivalents are already in use, these have been indicated, e.g. court sizes and marking for various games.

larger indoor area for physical activities of various kinds. These sports halls are purpose-built to permit the playing indoors of vigorous games and games practices without danger of damaging the structure or defacing the building in any way. They are usually 110 feet to 120 feet long, 60 feet to 90 feet wide and 20 feet to 30 feet high. This provision makes it possible to play tennis, basketball, badminton, netball and volleyball indoors on full size courts, in addition to providing suitable facilities for practising golf, cricket, fencing, judo, gymnastics and other indoor sports. Usually well lit and adequately heated, the sports hall provides a congenial indoor teaching space which enables a large variety of activities to be conducted indoors, and also makes it possible for regular coaching and practice, even in bad weather, of those activities which are normally only possible out-of-doors in good weather.

Teachers may expect to be consulted from time to time with regard to the provision and planning of sports halls, or may be required to indicate their requirements and preferences. In such cases it would be necessary for teachers to consider their own ideas on such features as:

a Siting

The physical relationship between the sports hall and the main school buildings is as important as its relationship to the changing facilities, the playing fields and the hard play areas.

b Size

This will of course depend greatly on the capital cost limits imposed, but a minimum playing area of 110 feet by 60 feet is recommended. This will permit tennis to be played on a full-size court (though a length of 120 feet would be more desirable) and netball to be played on a full-size court which is 100 feet long and 50 feet wide. Other indoor games requiring smaller pitches – for example, badminton, volleyball and basketball – are, of course, also possible.

c Height

A clear height of 25 feet (minimum) is required to permit the playing of such games as basketball, volleyball and badminton. It should be noted, however, that a clear height of 30 feet is required for the playing of top level adult badminton and it is an advantage if at least one sports hall of this height is available in each area.

30

d Floor

Many experiments have been conducted in an attempt to discover the most suitable floor surface for sports halls. Different materials have their own particular advantages but it has proved difficult, if not impossible, to find the ideal surface which is at one and the same time inexpensive, durable, resilient, non-slip, easily maintained, easily cleaned, and attractive in appearance.

Individual preference must be exercised in making a choice between so many possibilities and alternatives which include wood, tarmacadam, 'Bituturf', 'Rubberoid', 'Rub-kor', 'Sporteze', cork, 'Granwood', asphalt, P.V.C., and several other rubberised and plastic materials.

e Walls

It is advisable to have the maximum amount of playing area on both end and side walls. This playing surface should be hard and smooth without any projections and it is suggested that it should extend from the floor to a minimum height of 15 feet. The outside surface of the walls can provide a most valuable playing facility out-of-doors if the hard play-court adjoins it. The walls must be planned carefully in relation to the source of natural light.

f Lighting

The importance of adequate lighting cannot be over-emphasised. The problem is to avoid dazzle or glare while still providing sufficient light.

NATURAL LIGHTING

Diffused roof lighting is probably the most satisfactory, but may need to be supplemented by clerestory windows. Windows on end walls are not recommended, and if included on side walls they should be at least 15 feet from the floor. In order to avoid glare from direct sunlight it is advisable not to site them on south- or west-facing walls.

ARTIFICIAL LIGHTING

Protected strip lighting on the ceiling is probably the most satisfactory for general purposes, but it will be necessary to supplement this for special purposes, for example, additional groups or batteries of lamps, fixed or portable, at the sides of badminton courts and above the cricket nets or the boxing ring. It is an advantage to arrange for only a few lights to be controlled by the same switch so that only those lights really required are switched on at any one time.

g Ceiling

The design of the ceiling is closely associated with the problems of lighting. Any surface which does not transmit natural light should itself be light in colour. The roof should be insulated and planned in such a way that noise (from rain) and condensation are avoided.

h Heating

Sports halls must be heated to a level equivalent to that of a gymnasium (i.e. 55° F). The building is a teaching space and should therefore be attractive and congenial – although it will be used for strenuous activities, it will also be used for demonstration and coaching purposes, for lectures, and frequently to accommodate spectators. Adequate heating is essential and this is best supplied in the form of warm air blown in at floor level. Care must be taken to ensure that heating units are not noisy when in use because of the consequent interference with teaching and play. Overhead heating of such large areas has proved to be completely unsatisfactory. There are obvious advantages if it is possible to heat the sports hall and the adjoining changing facilities independently of the remainder of the school buildings when these facilities are being used outside normal school hours, especially at weekends or during school holidays.

i Ventilation

For most of the year the provision of satisfactory heating is the main problem, but there are times when some form of ventilation is required and this is probably most satisfactorily provided by extractor fans at a high level.

j Storage

The amount of equipment used in connection with the many games and activities conducted in a sports hall is considerable and generous storage facilities are an essential requirement. A minimum storage space of 300 square feet is considered necessary and a height of 8 feet to 9 feet is recommended to permit easy storage and moving of large items such as trampolines, games posts and gymnastics equipment. Shelves are required for the storage of small equipment, and cup-

32

boards which can be locked for the safe storage of valuables and personal items. Access doors to store-rooms must be at least 8 feet wide and 7 feet 6 inches high to facilitate the moving of equipment in and out of the store.

k Floor markings

When permanent markings are provided on the floor, the siting of pitches is of great importance. Too many markings can be confusing but it is interesting to note how little interference to playing any one particular game is caused by the fact that other pitches are marked in different colours on the same area. It is possible to provide permanent markings for about four games (for example, netball, basketball, badminton and volleyball) without causing much confusion. If a tennis court is required, it is probably sufficient to mark corners and junctions only in permanent markings and, when necessary, to mark out the rest of the court with adhesive tape which is easily removable. Permanent markings for tennis might, with advantage, be provided in certain sports halls on a regional basis rather than in every sports hall.

There is such a demand for markings for a number of different games in sports halls that some of the governing bodies of sport have recommended that uniformity of colour should be established for particular games. It has been suggested, for example, that court markings for basketball should be in orange or bright red and for badminton in white. This principle of uniformity has obvious advantages, but in all cases the choice of colour used will, of necessity, be influenced by the type and colour of the floor surface.

The courts for most games will be marked centrally on the playing area and several diagrams have been included to show typical floor marking arrangements (see Figs 4, 5, 6 and 7). For convenience and easy reference, court sizes have been indicated on additional diagrams which illustrate the official court markings for several games (see Figs 8, 9, 10, 11, 12 and 13).

l Siting of badminton courts

It is possible to mark four or more badminton courts according to the size of the playing area, and their siting should be a matter for careful consideration. The courts are often marked across the hall, parallel to the end walls (see Fig. 14), but if they are marked parallel to the side walls it is possible for the cricket or golf nets to be in use in one half of the hall while badminton or other activities are in progress in the other half. There are times when this is a distinct advantage (see Fig. 15). Additional advantages of this arrangement are that any natural light from the side walls will not adversely affect the game and if necessary extra batteries of lights can be fixed permanently to the side walls for use when badminton is being played.

m Practice courts

It is possible to play practice games of many kinds across the hall by making use of the existing permanent markings. Figures 14 and 15 on pages 51 and 53 indicate alternative suggestions for utilising permanent badminton court markings to provide practice courts suitable for basketball, netball and many minor games. There are several ways of arranging practice courts for volleyball by fixing floor sockets for the posts in suitable positions. In order to make the fullest use of existing court markings, the arrangement suggested in Fig. 16 on page 55 is perhaps the most convenient – it is certainly very effective. This arrangement makes use of existing netball court markings to provide three practice areas for volleyball by the provision of only two additional floor sockets. Figure 17 shows how easily temporary markings for a volleyball court could be provided within a sector of a permanently marked netball court.

n Floor sockets

Much successful experimental work has been carried out in connection with the provision of satisfactory sockets for games posts in sports halls. Posts without sockets are cumbersome because to be stable they require very heavy bases which are often difficult to move. Sockets are therefore considered to be essential and recent developments in the design of multi-purpose sockets and posts have been very successful. Much inconvenience and confusion can be avoided if all the sockets used are identical. In such a situation care must be taken to ensure that the base of each post used will fit the sockets exactly and since posts for different games are of varying dimensions, a modification to the base of the posts is sometimes necessary. Several firms now manufacture satisfactory multi-purpose games posts and sockets.

The siting of the sockets is of the greatest importance and a plan showing the exact position of all sockets in relation to the court markings is essential for each sports hall project. For some games (e.g. netball and badminton) the posts have to be located on the court perimeter lines. For other games (e.g. tennis and volleyball) the posts are situated at various distances outside the actual playing area. Exact details required for the siting of the sockets for the courts normally marked in sports halls are shown in Figs 8 (badminton), 9 (netball), 12 (volleyball), and 13 (tennis). Figure 19 indicates the location of all the floor sockets required if a sports hall is marked in accordance with the lay-out of courts suggested in Fig. 4 on page 37 and the practice areas suggested in Fig. 16 on page 55. (Modifications would, of course, be required if any other plans for permanent court markings were to be used.) This type of diagram will be required by the architect when the floor sockets have to be fixed.

o Golf and cricket nets

Most sports halls are fitted with netting to provide practice bays for cricket and golf. Care in siting these must be taken, not only to ensure adequate protection for players using the nets and others who might be working in different parts of the sports hall, but also to protect the fabric and fittings of the building itself. The golf bays require netting which has a smaller mesh than is needed for cricket, and cricket bays require additional protection at the batting end (white canvas sheeting or other suitable material). This sheeting is attached to the netting behind and on each side of the batsman to a height of about six feet and is needed to protect players in adjoining bays and to prevent balls from bouncing back from an adjacent wall.

The nets should be easily retractable so that when not in use they can be either drawn back to the end walls or raised up to the roof in order to leave the floor space clear for other activities. Nets which draw back to the end walls should overlap at the centre when in use, to ensure maximum safety. A roof netting at least 15 feet high is required over each of the bays. Cricket and golf practice nets which satisfy these basic requirements have been designed by many firms and the type used will be determined by personal preference.

The most usual arrangement in the normal 60 feet wide school sports hall is to provide two bays of netting each approximately 11 feet wide, extending the full length of the hall. One half of each bay is constructed in golf netting and the other half in cricket netting, with an overlap of at least 6 feet at the centre. For safety purposes there should be a space of at least 3 feet between the side wall and the nearest side net, and 6 feet between the end wall and the ends of each bay. A space of at least one foot is required between the inside side netting and the retractable basketball backboards to permit easy movement of the net and the backboards. If this inside netting can

(text is continued on page 60)

Figure 4 shows the perimeter court markings for:

a   Netball – shown — — — —— — —
b   Basketball – shown — · — · — ·
c   Volleyball – shown ....
d   4 Badminton courts – shown ——————
e   Tennis – corners and junctions only shown thus:

⌐   ┬   ¬

EXPLANATORY NOTES

1   All courts except badminton are sited centrally.
2   Badminton courts are sited lengthwise – 6 ft from each side wall with 8 ft between the inner side lines and 8 ft from each end wall with 16 ft between the inner base lines.
The advantages of siting the badminton courts lengthwise are:
a   Where cricket/golf nets are provided it is possible to play badminton in one half of the hall and at the same time use the cricket/golf nets in the other half.
b   Extra batteries of lights for use during badminton matches can be permanently sited on the side walls.
c   Natural lighting on the side walls can be provided without adversely affecting play on the badminton courts.
3   Care must be taken that the golf/cricket nets (sited lengthwise in one half of the hall) when in use are clear of the basketball backboards, which are normally retractable.
4   Five- or six-a-side football can be played on the netball court. The side lines of the netball court need not be used if it is decided that the side walls constitute part of the playing area.

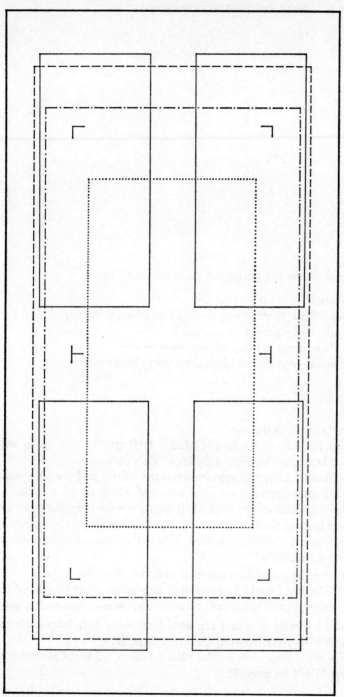

Scale $\frac{1}{20}''$=1ft

FIGURE 5   *Sports hall (alternative markings)*

Figure 5 shows the perimeter court markings for:

a   Netball – shown — — — — — — —
b   Basketball – shown — . — . — (see note (c) below)
c   Volleyball – shown ....
d   4 Badminton courts – shown ─────────
e   Tennis – corners and junctions only shown thus:

    ⌐   ┬   ┐

EXPLANATORY NOTES

1   The badminton courts are sited 7 ft from the side walls with 6 ft between the inner side lines. This permits:
a   additional marginal area between the courts and the side walls.
b   additional spectator space, if required, along the side walls.
c   the side lines of the basketball court to coincide with the outer side lines of the badminton courts, which reduces the amount of permanent marking required. Where the lines coincide there are two alternatives:
i) The lines could be retained as badminton markings.
ii) The lines could be marked in alternative short lengths of the badminton and basketball colours, e.g. ▬▬▬ ▭▭▭ ▬▬▬ ▭▭▭ ▬
2   The badminton courts are sited lengthwise 8 ft from each end wall with 16 ft between the inner base lines.
3   For other comments on this plan see notes 1, 3 and 4 accompanying Fig. 4 on page 37.

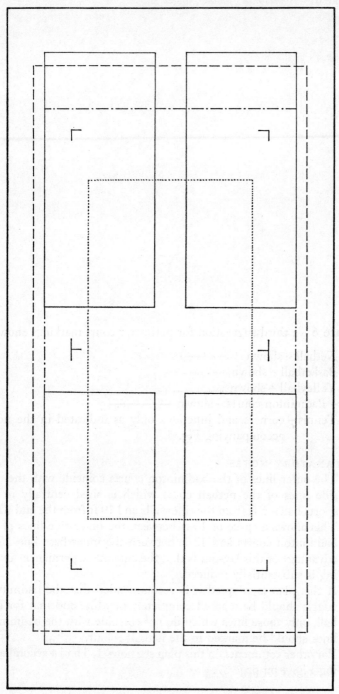

Scale $\frac{1}{20}'' = 1\,\text{ft}$

FIGURE 6   *Sports hall (another suggestion)*

Figure 6 – a third suggestion for perimeter court markings shows:

a   Netball – shown — — — — — —
b   Basketball – shown — . — . —
c   Volleyball – shown ....
d   4 Badminton courts – shown ——————
e   Tennis – corners and junctions only as indicated in the notes
       accompanying Fig. 5.

EXPLANATORY NOTES

1   The outer lines of the badminton courts coincide with the out-
     side lines of the netball court which is sited centrally in the
     sports hall – 5 ft from the side walls and 10 ft from the end walls.
     This allows a space of 10 ft between the inner side lines of the
     badminton courts and 12 ft between the inner base lines. The
     advantage of this lay-out is that the amount of permanent mark-
     ing is substantially reduced.
     If this plan is adopted it is recommended that the badminton
     courts should be marked completely in white and that for net-
     ball, only those lines which do not coincide with the badminton
     lines should be marked in the netball colour.

2   For other comments on this plan see notes 1, 3 and 4 accompany-
     ing Fig. 4 on page 37.

40

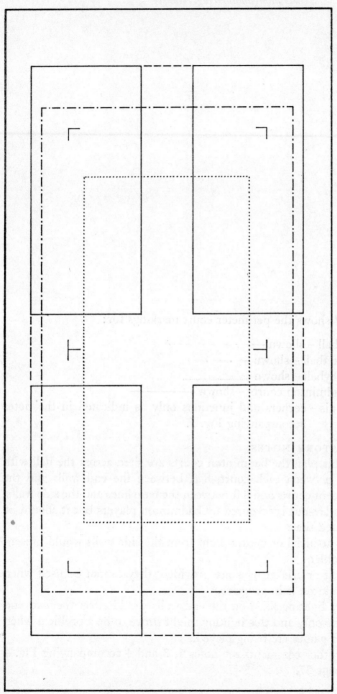

Scale $\frac{1}{20}'' = 1$ft

FIGURE 7 *Sports hall (another suggestion)*

Figure 7 shows the perimeter court markings for:

a Netball – shown — — —— — —

b Basketball – shown — · — · —

c Volleyball – shown ....

d 4 Badminton courts – shown ——————

e Tennis – corners and junctions only as indicated in the notes accompanying Fig. 5.

EXPLANATORY NOTES

1 In this plan the badminton courts are sited across the hall with 8 ft between each court, 8 ft between the end walls and the adjacent courts and 8 ft between the base lines and the side walls. This lay-out is favoured by badminton players but it should be realised that:

a Any artificial or natural light from the side walls would present a problem.

b If golf or cricket bays are provided, they cannot be used when badminton is in progress.

c Extra lighting fixed on the end walls would affect the two end courts only and this lighting might prove to be a problem when other games are being played.

2 For other comments see notes 1, 3 and 4 accompanying Fig. 4 on page 37.

42

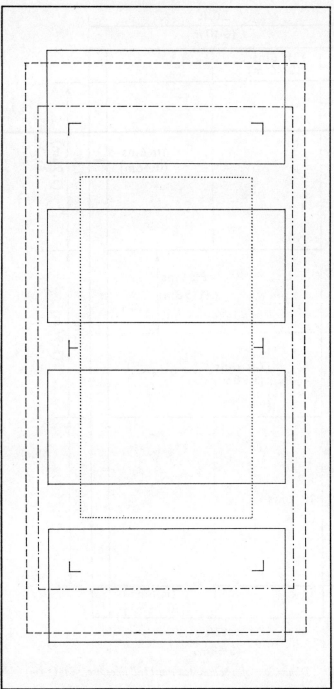

Scale $\frac{1}{20}''$=1ft

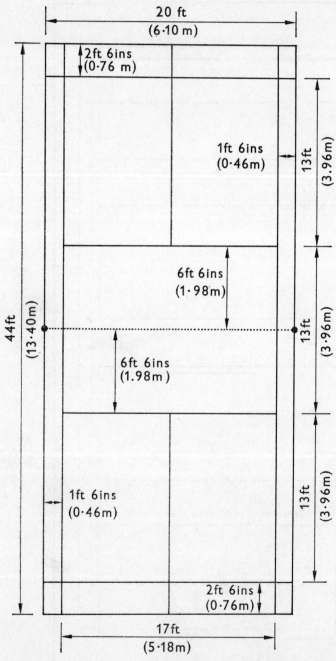

FIGURE 8   *Dimensions of a badminton court (all lines are 2 ins (5 cm) wide)*

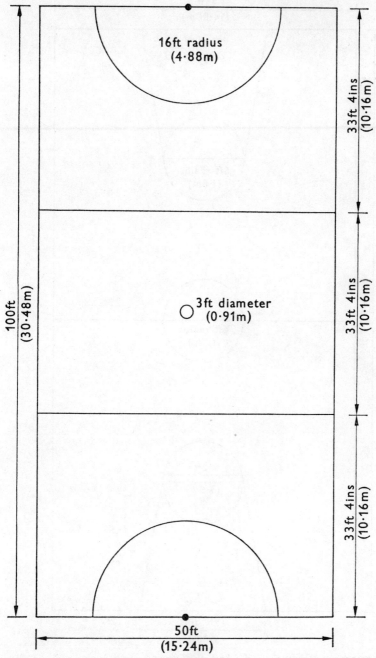

FIGURE 9   *Dimensions of a netball court*

45

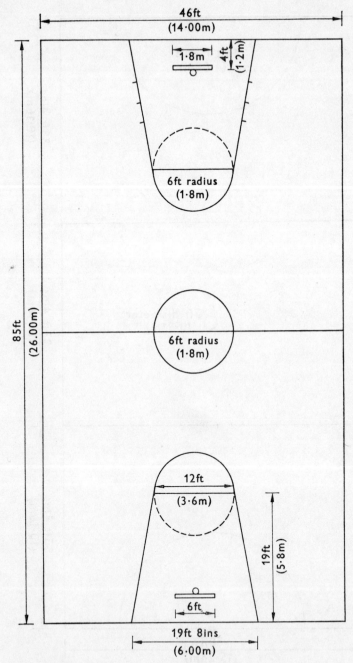

FIGURE 10   *Dimensions of a basketball court*

46

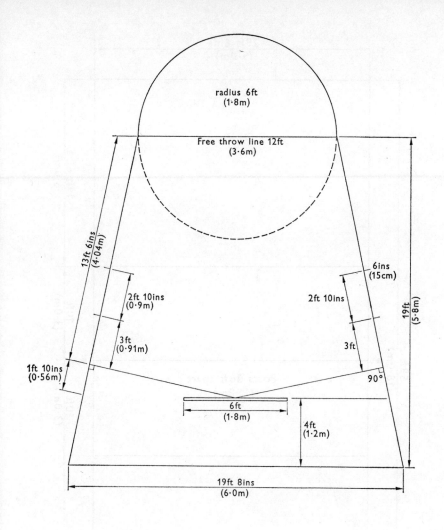

radius 6ft
(1·8m)

Free throw line 12ft
(3·6m)

13ft 6ins
(4·04m)

6ins
(15cm)

2ft 10ins
(0·9m)

2ft 10ins

3ft
(0·91m)

3ft

1ft 10ins
(0·56m)

90°

19ft
(5·8m)

6ft
(1·8m)

4ft
(1·2m)

19ft 8ins
(6·0m)

FIGURE II   *Basketball – details of the restricted area (the free throw lane)*

47

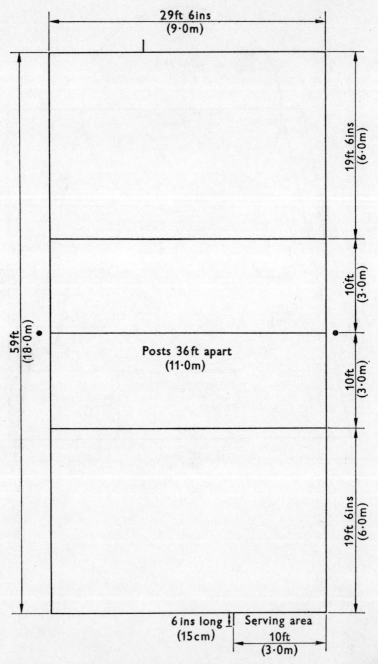

FIGURE 12 *Dimensions of a volleyball court (note: a minimum of 10 m is recommended between posts)*

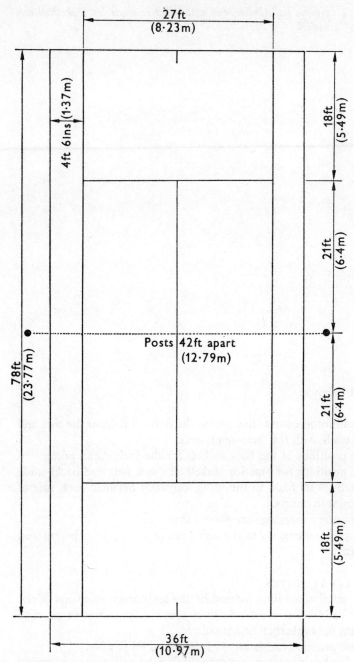

27ft
(8·23m)

4ft 6Ins (1·37m)

18ft
(5·49m)

21ft
(6·4m)

Posts 42ft apart
(12·79m)

21ft
(6·4m)

78ft
(23·77m)

18ft
(5·49m)

36ft
(10·97m)

FIGURE 13   *Dimensions of a tennis court*

49

FIGURE 14 *Sports hall (badminton with practice areas for basketball and netball)*

Figure 14 shows:

a   4 badminton courts sited across the hall – 8 ft from the side and end walls with 8 ft between courts.

b   The positions of the floor sockets for the badminton posts.

c   The positions for practice basketball rings, nets and backboards (6 ft by 4 ft) fixed to the walls, centrally between each pair of badminton courts.

d   Temporary markings are shown thus . . .
They are extensions of the side lines of each pair of badminton courts.

EXPLANATORY NOTES

1   The continuous lines formed by the temporary extension of the four badminton court side lines provide two effective practice courts for basketball or netball.

2   These practice courts are 60 ft long and 48 ft wide.

3   For further comments see notes 3(a), 3(b) and 4 accompanying Fig. 15 on page 53.

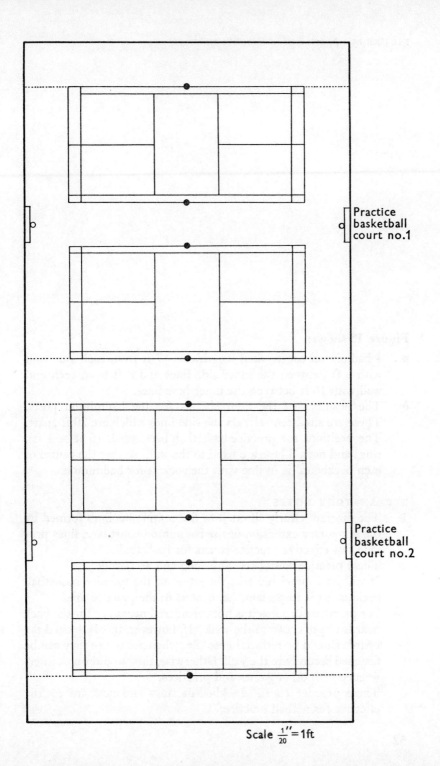

Practice
basketball
court no.1

Practice
basketball
court no.2

Scale $\frac{1''}{20}$ = 1ft

FIGURE 15   *Sports hall (alternative markings)*

Figure 15 shows:

a   4 badminton courts sited lengthwise – 7 ft from each side wall
with 6 ft between the inner side lines and 8 ft from each end
wall with 16 ft between the inner base lines.

b   The positions of the floor sockets for the badminton posts.
These are sited centrally on the side lines which are 20 ft apart.

c   The positions for practice basketball backboards (6 ft × 4 ft),
rings and nets. These are fixed to the walls so that the centre of
each backboard is in line with the sockets for badminton.

EXPLANATORY NOTES

1   The diagram clearly shows how the continuous lines formed by
the temporary extension of the badminton court base lines provide two effective practice courts for basketball.

2   These practice courts are 60 ft long and 44 ft wide.

3*a*   It will be appreciated that the siting of the practice basketball
backboards is important, i.e. central to the practice area.

 b   For practice purposes it is not considered necessary for the back
boards to project from the wall. If, however, this is desired the
boards should be retractable so that when not in use they can be
fastened securely to the wall. Otherwise, they would cause interference with other games and practices.

4   These practice courts, backboards rings and nets are equally
effective for netball practice.

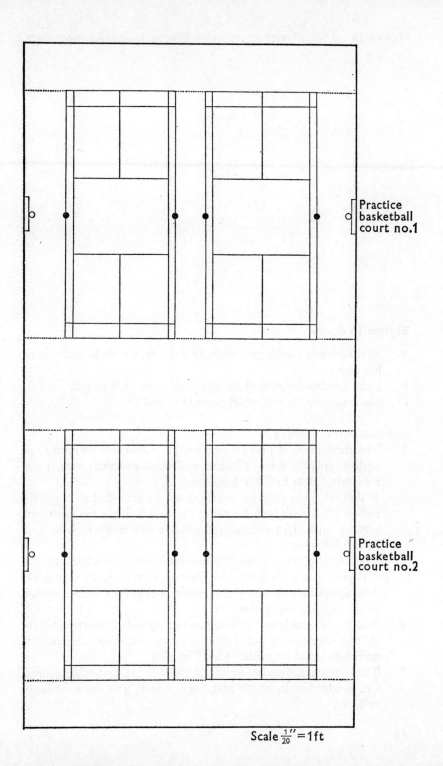

Practice basketball court no.1

Practice basketball court no.2

Scale $\frac{1}{20}'' = 1$ ft

FIGURE 16   *A netball court provides three effective volleyball practice areas*

Figure 16 shows:

a   Netball court markings – excluding the centre circle and shooting area.
b   Floor sockets for netball or volleyball posts at A and B.
c   Floor sockets for volleyball posts at C and D.

EXPLANATORY NOTES
1   The three areas of play formed by the cross-court markings for netball provide three effective volleyball practice areas, each measuring 50 ft by 33 ft 4 ins.
2   If desired these practice courts could be extended to approximately 60 ft in length by using the side walls as the base and serving lines. (An official volleyball court is 59 ft long and 29 ft 6 ins wide.)
3   The nets for these three practice areas can be fastened to the volleyball posts placed in the floor sockets at A, B, C and D. The advantages of this arrangement is that four posts, instead of six, support three nets.
4   Additional markings for these practice volleyball courts are considered unnecessary but if desired for special reasons temporary markings could be made. (See Fig. 17.)
5   These practice areas are equally suitable for playing other games, e.g. padder tennis, skittle ball, rugby touch, grid areas for football, etc.

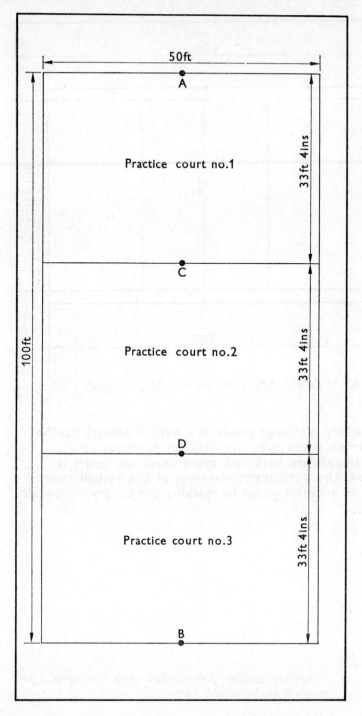

50ft

A

Practice court no.1

33ft 4ins

C

100ft

Practice court no.2

33ft 4ins

D

Practice court no.3

33ft 4ins

B

Scale $\frac{1''}{20}$ = 1ft

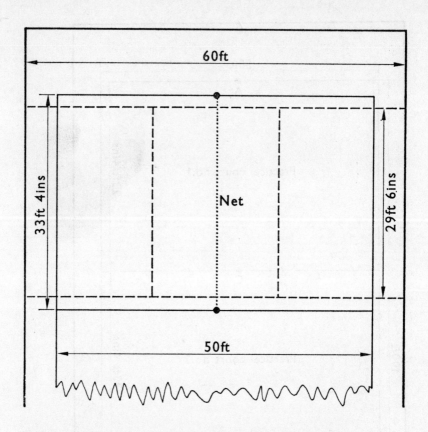

Temporary markings inside the netball sectors can be put down when special volleyball practices or tournaments are held and more than one court is needed. The permanent markings of the netball court serve as a useful guide in marking temporary volleyball courts.

FIGURE 17 *Temporary markings for volleyball inside a sector of a permanently marked netball court*

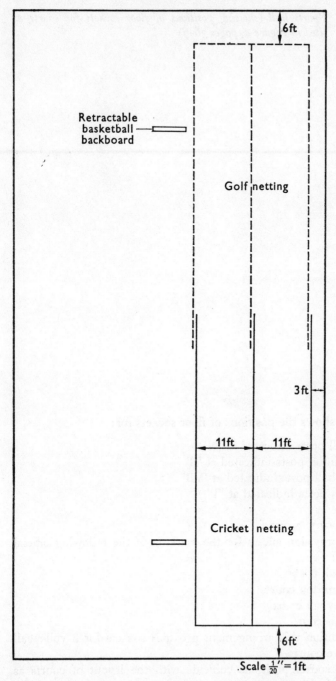

6ft

Retractable
basketball
backboard

Golf netting

3ft

11ft   11ft

Cricket netting

6ft

Scale $\frac{1}{20}$″=1ft

FIGURE 18   *Sports hall (showing location of cricket and golf bays)*

Figure 19 shows the positions of floor sockets for:

a Netball posts indicated at 'NB'
b Badminton posts indicated at 'B'
c Volleyball posts indicated at 'VB'
d Tennis posts indicated at 'T'

EXPLANATORY NOTES
1 This provision allows for the marking of the following official courts:
1 netball court
4 badminton courts
1 volleyball court
1 tennis court
2 In addition this arrangement provides sockets for 3 volleyball practice courts.
3 These socket positions coincide with the layout of courts as shown in Fig. 4.

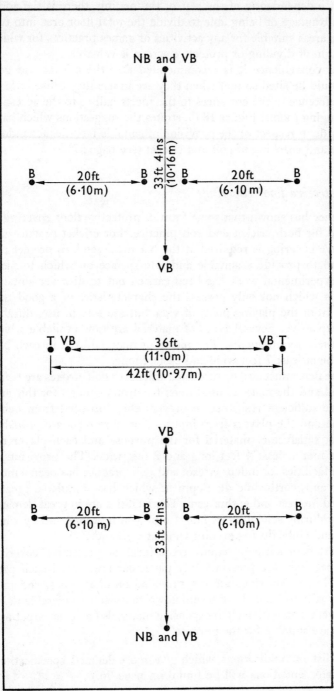

Scale $\frac{1}{20}'' = $ 1ft.

be used independently of the rest of the netting, there is the additional advantage of being able to divide the total floor area into two practice areas suitable for any activities or games practices for which some form of dividing or protective screen is valuable.

For convenience it is recommended that the cricket and golf nets should be sited so that when they are in use they cause little or no interference to the entrances to the sports hall or to the access to the changing rooms. Figure 18 illustrates the suggestions which have been made in respect of the provision of suitable facilities for indoor practice and coaching of golf and cricket (see page 57).

p Protective floor coverings

Experience has shown that some form of protective floor covering is required for both cricket and golf practice. For cricket practice the protective covering is required at the batsman's end, to protect the floor and to provide a suitable and safe surface on which to play. Much experimental work has been carried out to discover suitable materials which not only possess the characteristics of a good turf surface from the playing point of view but are safe in use, durable and inexpensive. Several types of material are now available which satisfy these requirements. The pieces of material used in each bay should be at least 7 feet wide and 24 feet long.

The floor must also be protected whenever golf strokes are being practised and the material used must be strong enough for this and still have sufficient resilience to prevent the club used from being damaged and the players from injury. Coir fibre mats are probably the most satisfactory material for the purpose and each player requires a mat at least 4 feet long and 2 feet wide. The provision of suitable facilities for indoor cricket and golf practice has been a most popular and worthwhile development which has stimulated greatly increased interest and enthusiasm. The facilities are in great demand not only during school hours but also by youth groups and by adult classes and clubs during evenings and at weekends.

Most floor surfaces require some form of protective covering when spectators are present. Only particular areas need such protection, but if coverings are not provided outdoor shoes, and particularly stiletto heels, have been known to cause considerable damage. Several comparatively inexpensive materials (such as carpet and canvas) are suitable for the purpose.

(A list of publications which give more detailed specifications and recommendations will be found on page 96.)

12   Special allowances for equipment

The expansion of the physical education programme has made it necessary for local education authorities to provide equipment on a generous scale for a very wide range of physical activities. Authorities normally include in their annual estimates a sum of money for each school, usually calculated on a per capita basis, for

a   the provision and repair of equipment for games and athletics;
b   affiliation fees to county and national schools sports associations;
c   special equipment for outdoor pursuits and school clubs;
d   travelling expenses for school teams and hospitality for visiting teams.

The allowances for these items vary from authority to authority and also according to the size of the school and the age of the pupils. A secondary school of 500 pupils might have an allowance varying between £200 and £400, while a large comprehensive school might be allowed as much as £1,000. This allowance is usually available in addition to other funds for the provision, inspection, repair and maintenance of gymnastic equipment. Some authorities, realising the value of a comprehensive inter-school and inter-area sports programme and the excellent work of the school sports associations, give financial assistance not only to district but also to county school sports associations.

13   School sports and games associations

The improvement in facilities for sport and the expansion of the programme of physical education in schools have been reflected in the widening of the range of activities conducted by school sports and games associations. It is now quite common to find these associations including in their various sectional activities not only rugby and association football, cricket, athletics, swimming, netball and hockey but also badminton, basketball, tennis, table-tennis, trampolining, sailing, canoeing and orienteering. Much of this expansion of activities is a direct result of the additional indoor facilities which have become available through the provision of sports halls.

The organisation of all these activities demands a great deal of time and effort on the part of teachers, whose services, either in an administrative capacity or in practical work, coaching, refereeing and supervising, are given quite freely during out-of-school hours without any material reward. Tribute must be paid to the excellent work done by so many teachers whose voluntary efforts are responsible for this extremely valuable contribution to the social development and physical welfare of their pupils. The value of this work is not limited to the pupil's school life. Education, including physical education, provides something for the present and something for the future for each individual, and there is no doubt that the carry-over value into post-school life of the experiences gained in school clubs and in the inter-school and inter-area games programmes is considerable.

14 National coaching schemes

The appointment of national coaches for various sports and the establishment of national coaching schemes has been of particular value to both men and women teachers. The English Football Association and the Amateur Athletics Association were pioneers in this development and many of the governing bodies of sport have now appointed experienced and well-qualified specialist staff who are available to conduct coaching courses for teachers, leaders and pupils.

It is now possible to obtain the services of national coaches, not only for football and athletics but also for swimming, hockey, basketball, tennis, table-tennis, gymnastics, netball, rugby, golf, judo, canoeing, cricket and so on, and there is no doubt that the continuing improvement in standards of performance in all these sports, at all levels, is a reflection of the successful work of the national coaches and of the national coaching schemes. The availability of advanced coaching has resulted in the adoption of new and more efficient techniques, more effective methods of fitness training, a more scientific and individual approach to coaching, new tactics in team play, greater enthusiasm and more participation and competition at all levels.

15 Joint provision of facilities for sport and recreation

An important recent development which will greatly influence the curriculum of physical education in secondary schools is the ever-increasing number of projects for the joint provision of facilities for sport and recreation. It is the statutory obligation of local education authorities to provide facilities for physical education for the children in the schools. Local authorities, that is the rural and urban district councils, and borough and county borough councils, have the statutory obligation to provide recreational facilities for the general public. These latter facilities, which include public parks, swimming baths, golf courses, playing fields, running tracks, and so on, are provided for the use of the general public, either in junior or adult clubs, in league or non-league competition, or for individual recreation. These facilities are also available for use by youth organisations and in many instances by schools, though the priorities for use are adults, youths and then schools.

The facilities provided by the local education authorities have exactly the reverse priorities; the school hall, gymnasium, swimming bath, playing fields, changing rooms and other recreational facilities are primarily for the use of the children of the school, then for clubs connected with the school, then for youth organisations and for instructional classes organised by the education department, and lastly for adult organisations and clubs and the general public.

What is not always clearly understood is that the amount of money allowed by the Department of Education and Science for the building of a school is only just sufficient to provide the facilities required by the school itself. In other words, only the minimum number of indoor teaching spaces needed by the school, only the minimum number of playing pitches, only the minimum amount of changing space can be provided, and there is no way in which the local education authority, by itself, can provide more.

Another fact which is often overlooked is that the principle of joint use is not new. With very few exceptions it is the declared policy of local education authorities to permit the use of their school facilities by outside organisations during out-of-school hours. Many local council playing fields, tennis courts and swimming baths are used by schools during school hours. Though permission to grant the use of school facilities to outside organisations is in the power of school managers or governors, there are often very good reasons why the facilities provided do not adequately cope with the demands for adult and community use. For example, the main reason why most school playing fields cannot be used by outside organisations is that this would mean over-use and the pitches would very soon be out-of-use to everyone. This becomes obvious when one accepts the facts that in the first place only minimum provision for the needs of the school itself has been made, and in the second place pitches are often over-used by the school.

The difficulties which local councils face in providing a sufficient number of playing pitches for adult use are increased by the need to provide adequate changing, washing and social facilities for those who use the pitches. All these items are very costly and it is gradually being recognised that it is more sensible and economical for local councils and local education authorities to cooperate in joint planning, joint provision and joint use of such facilities. School gymnasia are often used by clubs for occasional training and coaching sessions or for regular club use. On the other hand the school gymnasium and assembly hall are not ideal places for adult badminton, basketball, or volleyball; they were not planned for such purposes, and not many local councils have, in the past, provided suitable facilities. Fortunately the sports halls now being built at many schools will be much more suitable for such activities. It has become abundantly clear not only to local education authorities, to local councils and to sports organisations, but also to the general public that all the facilities required cannot be afforded in duplicate – one set for school use only and another set for out-of-school use. Joint planning and provision for joint use is both economically sound and common sense, and more and more facilities are being provided by the combined efforts of education committees and local councils. By such joint effort, many school facilities are being planned with the needs of the community as well as of the school in mind and of course the school benefits greatly from the increased provision being made. Changing facilities are able to be enlarged and improved, sports halls can be made larger and higher, spectator accommodation and facilities for refreshments can be provided, storage space for equipment can be increased, flood-lighting for outdoor facilities such as all-weather pitches and running tracks can be provided and in many cases a swimming bath which could not otherwise be afforded becomes a possibility. Great enterprise has been shown by many local councils who have provided or are planning to provide sports centres which include swimming pools, multi-purpose sports halls of varying sizes, squash courts, gymnasia, special rooms for fencing and weight training, committee rooms, lecture halls, refreshment and spectator accommodation together with outdoor grass and all-weather playing areas, hard play courts and running tracks. Many of these sports centres have been planned and provided jointly by local councils, local education authorities, industry and voluntary organisations. A recent trend which may become a very important development in the future is the planning of sports centres for combined school and community use, sited centrally in relation to the schools and the community, so that physical education facilities required by one or more schools are provided and recreational needs of the area met.

The availability of such improved facilities for both outdoor and indoor activity will greatly affect the pattern, the content and the planning of the physical education programmes of the schools. Joint planning and joint provision offer distinct advantages and may often be the means of providing valuable facilities in areas where such facilities would otherwise be on a much less generous scale or even non-existent.

Physical education teachers in the future will be able to plan their programmes not only with their own school's facilities in mind but also with the knowledge that in many areas improved local facilities will permit greater opportunities for the expansion of the curriculum.

16 The Sports Council

The tremendous interest recently aroused with regard to the provision of facilities for sport and recreation has been in no small measure due to the establishment of the National Sports Council. This was set up to advise the government on the facilities needed in the country for physical recreation, on the standards of provision to be aimed at, on matters relating to the development of amateur sport and physical recreation and to foster cooperation among the statutory authorities and voluntary organisations. The work of the Sports Council is concerned with making suggestions and recommendations on the following main topics:

a   the primary needs of the community for physical recreation;
b   the standard and scale of provision required;
c   the joint provision and joint use of facilities;
d   training and coaching for sport and recreation;
e   priorities in sports development;
f   assistance to international amateur teams competing overseas;
g   finance;
h   research.

To enable the council to conduct its work more efficiently, four committees have been formed:

The International Committee   advises on the development of amateur international sport and makes recommendations concerning applications for financial assistance to international teams competing abroad.
The Facilities Planning Committee   advises on matters relating to the improvement and provision of facilities for physical recreation and

sport particularly where public expenditure is involved, through the powers and responsibilities of government departments.

The Research and Statistics Committee advises on matters of research, particularly in the fields of sociology, sports medicine and physiology, and the documentation of material relating to these and any other aspects of sport.

The Sports Development and Coaching Committee is concerned with the general development of sport and advises on the policy and procedure for grants towards capital expenditure for facilities and other expenses connected with the administration, organisation and coaching of sport.

To assist the Sports Council in its work and to ensure that the more local needs of the country are given maximum consideration, regional sports councils have also been established. The greater part of the work of the regional sports councils is undertaken by three main committees.

The Technical Panel, acting on information provided by project sub-committees and with the help of experts from a wide variety of statutory bodies and voluntary organisations, gives help and advice locally regarding any projects for the provision of facilities for sport and recreation and advises the Sports Council with regard to the viability or otherwise of proposed projects.

The Water Recreation Sub-Committee advises on the use and development of rivers, lakes, reservoirs, canals and coastal areas for recreational purposes.

The Joint Study Group is concerned with studying the problems of and advising on the joint planning and joint use of facilities for sport.

Regional sports councils are themselves assisted in their work by county sports federations and local sports advisory councils. The county sports federations consist of representatives of all county sports associations and are concerned with the scope and standards of provision and the use of facilities for sport in their areas. They not only make surveys and reports of existing facilities and of levels of participation but also of the facilities required, and they form a close link between those who provide facilities, those who advise on the provision of facilities, and those who use them. Local sports advisory councils provide the opportunity for local authorities, sports organisations, voluntary organisations and all connected with and interested in sport locally, to discuss the local situation with regard to facilities, the use of existing facilities and requirements for sport. Their main function is to endeavour to ensure the maximum use of all existing facilities and to advise the local authorities, the

66

county sports federations and the regional sports council with regard to the needs of the locality for additional facilities.

The tremendous work done by all these various bodies, giving, as they do, consideration to all aspects of the provision and use of facilities for sport and recreation at national, regional and local level, is showing some excellent results. Much more is already known and a great deal more will be known in the future about the use of existing facilities and about the needs for additional facilities. More important is the fact that as a result of so much effort, new facilities for indoor and outdoor sport of all kinds are being provided and planned throughout the country. As already stated, the principle of joint provision and dual use has been generally accepted and as a result there is little doubt that increased opportunities for participation in sport and recreation will be available in the future.

Such provision will greatly influence and help the development of physical education programmes in schools as well as the sporting and recreational activities of adults. Teachers interested in games or outdoor pursuits, and particularly specialists in physical education, should welcome any and every opportunity to be actively engaged in the work of local sports advisory councils, county sports federations and the committees of the regional sports councils. It is not sufficient for teachers to wait for others to do all that is necessary to provide suitable and adequate facilities; wherever possible they should themselves be part of and personally involved in the planning and the provision of all that is required.

Tribute must be paid to the excellent contribution made by the Central Council of Physical Recreation in the development of the work of the Sports Council. The officers of the C.C.P.R. at both central and regional level have borne by far the largest administrative and executive burden of the Sports Council's work and it is largely due to their energy, enthusiasm and efficiency that so much has been accomplished. The fact that the C.C.P.R. has now been officially incorporated into the Sports Council is a tribute to the effectiveness of the work that has been done. There is no doubt that the work and the influence of the Sports Council will have a profound impact on the future pattern of physical education in schools and of physical recreation and sport in the community.

17 The training of physical education teachers

The standard of physical education in schools, whilst being related to and influenced by the methods used, reflects most of all the standards of the teaching – the ability of the teacher. It would therefore be relevant to discuss, if only briefly, some recent changes in the pattern of teacher training.

The most important change has been the extension of the period of basic training from two to three years. In spite of the opportunities which were previously available for selected two-year trained teachers to attend a supplementary one-year course of specialist training, it must be acknowledged that the majority of teachers responsible for physical education in secondary schools were two-year trained only, with physical education as one of the main or advanced subjects studied. It follows, therefore, that since the introduction of the three-year course more recently qualified teachers who undertake the responsibility for physical education will have followed a longer course of study than was previously possible. Those responsible for the training of specialist teachers, however, seem to be agreed that the three-year course does not provide the opportunity for as comprehensive a training as was previously afforded by a two-year course of study followed by the supplementary and much more intensive one-year course. This contention is based on the calculation of time available for the subject. In other words a third of the time available during each year of a three-year course does not approximate to the total of a third of the time available during a two-year course plus a full year of specialist study. For many years before the introduction of the three-year basic course of training in 1960, a number of women's colleges offered three-year specialist courses of study in physical education. These colleges have now been incorporated into the national pattern in which the study of physical education as a main or advanced subject is part of the general three-year basic course of teacher training. For both men and women students, some colleges, because of their facilities and staff, offer what is called a *wing* course, which is often considered to be rather more advanced than a non-wing course.

It is not generally appreciated that a teacher who has completed the normal three-year course can, after a minimum of three years' satisfactory teaching experience, attend a supplementary course for a year, to follow a course of concentrated study in a subject which was not studied at main or advanced level during the initial three-year course of training. Many excellent physical education teachers have obtained their specialist qualification in this way.

The most recent development in teacher training, however, has been the introduction of a four-year course of study leading to the award of the degree of Bachelor of Education. In many colleges, physical education is one of the subjects which can be included in the course of study for this degree. It is expected that such graduates, whose four-year course of study includes the full three years of professional training for teaching, will prove to be a very valuable acquisition to the physical education profession.

Courses of advanced study which are available at some British universities include those leading to the award of a Diploma in Education, or a Diploma in Physical Education, or a Master of Education degree, and it is possible to include physical education as one of the subjects studied in the Bachelor of Arts degree course at the University of Birmingham. Degree courses in physical education are available at many American and Canadian universities and a number of specialist teachers from Britain have graduated in this way.

A trend in recent years has been for an increasing number of students and qualified teachers to pursue these various courses of advanced study. Such opportunity for extended study and the close links with universities and with university departments of education and physical education should, in due course, have a profound influence on the administration, the organisation and the practice of physical education in schools.

18 Research, tests and measurements

In recent years students of physical education have become increasingly aware of many scientific studies not only of growth and development but also of the anatomical and physiological aspects of exercise. The conclusions drawn from the considerable research undertaken, from the study of body types – somatotyping – and from conducting numerous and varied tests and measurements of many kinds, have served to emphasise the individuality of children from the physical viewpoint. Furthermore, philosophical, psychological and sociological studies have highlighted the individuality of children with regard to aptitudes and attitudes, mental, emotional and social. All this seems to lead to the conclusion that any teaching method, if it is to be satisfactory from the truly educational standpoint as distinct from the mere transference of information or the acquisition of skill, must cater for the varying aptitudes, abilities, attitudes and needs of individual pupils. Is it not reasonable to conclude that the information obtained from all the research being undertaken, and from all the tests being carried out and formulated, will prove this work to be no more than an academic exercise unless it has a bearing upon and a direct link with the teaching situation?

A number of publications are available dealing with these aspects of study and therefore comment in greater detail is unnecessary. The trend towards emphasising these facets of research in teacher training courses has been of great interest because if through research much has been discovered, then surely the findings should be reflected in teaching methods so that the basic aim can be achieved – to accommodate each individual irrespective of physique, physical ability and attitude. It is equally clear that such methods should develop individual talent to the full so that all pupils can experience, as frequently as possible, a sense of achievement.

19 Changes in teaching method

Research on the lines suggested above has also been conducted over many years in the practical field (that is, in the realistic teaching situation), to discover ways in which the fundamental educational principle of dealing with children as individuals can be satisfied. This research, by practising teachers, organisers, advisers and lecturers, has been directed towards an individual approach to teaching which:

a   allows opportunities for
   i) exploration and experimentation;
   ii) individual choice;
   iii) the exercise and development of creative ability;
   iv) the use of imagination;
   v) the development of independence, initiative and enterprise;
   vi) developing understanding and awareness; and

b   places children in problem-solving situations where
   i) a thought-process is involved;
   ii) the potential ability of each child can be developed to the full.

In these situations a sense of achievement comes within the experience of each individual who is thereby helped to achieve a degree of security, confidence and adequacy. Reference has already been made to the address given by Sir Ronald Gould, formerly General Secretary of the N.U.T., at a conference called by the Schools Council to consider 'The Educational Implications of Social and Economic Change' (1966). In his address he also said: 'It is not sufficient to train people to be able to do a job mechanically. It is necessary that they should know more about the underlying principles of the job which they are doing so that they can apply those principles to a completely new situation. So rote learning and purely mechanical training are really quite inadequate. We need a great number of people who are readily adaptable. To make people more adaptable children ought to be forced more and more into a position of discovering solutions to problems for themselves. They should be less spoon-fed; learning should be emphasised much more than teaching.'

How have these requirements been achieved?

They have been achieved in all aspects of physical education by virtually discarding regimental instruction and completely teacher-dominated techniques for the teaching of specific skills (*direct teaching*) in favour of a method which provides situations in which children are allowed to practise freely, to discover for themselves, to learn by exploration and to choose freely not only what they do but how they do it (*indirect teaching*). At other times they are allowed to practise and to choose quite freely within the limitations imposed upon them by the teacher (*limitation method*). In such situations the children are stimulated by the teacher to find their own individual solutions to the problems set, and it is important that teachers now realise that individual solutions to any problem may be very different from each other, but at the same time no less effective and acceptable. This acceptance is one of the most important features of the recent successful developments of new teaching methods and techniques.

How do these principles work out in practice in the different aspects of physical education?

In *swimming*, children are allowed to become familiar with the environment and confident in it by free play and free practice. Later, with the help of a variety of swimming aids such as arm bands, rings and floats, they are encouraged to find a way of moving and later to find other ways of moving in the water. The teacher becomes a coach and by careful observation and stimulation helps individuals to develop greater efficiency in those ways of moving which seem to be more natural for them. In other words, they try different ways and find the one that suits them best. This type of experimental approach has been most successful and has led to the much more general acceptance of the multi-stroke method of teaching swimming instead of the single-stroke method in which every child in the class is taught to swim by the basic stroke favoured by the teacher even if the particular stroke chosen does not suit the children. The aim in teaching swimming is to find a way of moving along the surface of the water. At the earliest stage the particular type of stroke used by the child is relatively unimportant. What is important is for each child to be able to find, as quickly as possible, a means of propulsion. Subsequent practice and coaching by the use of demonstration, observation and stimulation are directed towards an improvement in style and technique in the child's natural stroke, and later towards developing the ability to use other strokes successfully. Thus, as in gymnastics, the swimming lessons become a continuous process aimed at the development of individual quality and variety of performance.

Later, advanced work is introduced to include life-saving, survival swimming, sub-aqua technique and methods of resuscitation. The many awards of the Amateur Swimming Association, the Royal Life-Saving Society and the English Schools' Swimming Association have been modified and increased to present greater and more varied challenges of an objective character for children of all ages and abilities.

A very successful experiment in the teaching of swimming which has had an important impact on the organisation of swimming instruction is the *Midlothian Scheme*. The scheme was based on the premise that a series of daily swimming lessons over a comparatively short period would be more effective in teaching children to swim than the same number of lessons taken weekly. Experimental work using controlled groups was conducted whereby some classes attended the baths daily, except weekends, for a three-week period, while others attended weekly for fifteen weeks. The results proved that many more children learned to swim more quickly during the three-week period of daily lessons and only administrative difficulties have prevented the more universal acceptance and implementation of this method.

In *organised games* lessons, similar modifications in teaching methods have been made. In the early stages, as in swimming, the opportunity to play is recognised as of greater significance than the need or demand for the learning of specific techniques or skills. Young children are given opportunities to practise freely and to experiment with a wide variety of different types of games equipment. Thus they learn to catch, to throw, to field, to serve, to hit, to aim, to kick and so on in a wide variety of games situations, individually, in pairs, and in small groups or teams. The teacher coaches by the use of demonstration, observation, question and answer and stimulation to produce as much quality and variety as possible in each individual. Maximum participation and involvement for everyone is a major objective and teacher intervention, guidance or help increases with the developing ability of each child, group or class.

As ability develops and greater experience is gained, the teacher imposes individual, partner and small group tasks or practices based on the types of movements already mentioned (limitation method), thus ensuring that all children are given opportunities to try out a wide variety of games skills and practices. Simple small-side team games and simplified forms of major team games are introduced to supplement the individual, partner and small group practices, so that lessons could include both practices and competitive small-team games of skittle ball, rounders, stool-ball, football, cricket, hockey, netball, volleyball, badminton, batinton, padder tennis, basketball and many other minor and major games.

The basic methods of coaching in all games at both school and post-school levels have undergone revolutionary changes during the last few years. Such innovations as the grid system in football, group coaching in cricket, and class methods of coaching in badminton and table-tennis have made a great impact on general teaching methods during games lessons. At all ages and at all stages, even at adult level, the recent trends have been towards encouraging players to think for themselves, not only when developing individual skills but also when applying these skills in games situations and in cooperation with others. The teacher's task, as in gymnastics, is to create the situations in which a thought process is involved so that every practice and every game, whether at an elementary or advanced level, is a 'thinking' game. The success of such methods is reflected in the fact that small-side versions of major team games are recognised at all levels, including post-school, youth and adult, and accepted, in their own right, as part of a games programme. Five-a-side football and hockey, seven-a-side rugby and lacrosse, initially used as methods of ensuring maximum individual participation, are now recognised as official games and inter-house, inter-school and inter-club competitions in these games have been popular developments in recent years.

In a recent article, 'Keeping up with Educational Change', Tudor Powell Jones, now vice-principal of a college of education, wrote: 'Just as we are currently reviewing the subject matter for the curriculum to keep it in line with the increasing body of knowledge, teaching aids and methods should be constantly over-hauled in the light of newly available resources.

'It is very difficult to summarise all the new educational ideas which have emerged in the last decade, but there is some justification for claiming that the most prevalent and dominating of these principles have been those of discovery, integration and flexibility. It has been agreed by researchers and teachers that children learn best what comes to them pleasantly and as a personal discovery. It has become the teachers' duty to create an environment in which children can progress, and learning situations in which they learn to learn.'

Although special reference has been made to some of the modifications of teaching methods only in respect of swimming and organised games lessons, similar changes have taken place in the teaching of all other aspects of physical education. It is generally agreed, however, that the most revolutionary changes have taken place in the realms of dance and gymnastics.

20 Developments in the teaching of gymnastics

A study of the publications of the Board of Education (the syllabuses of 1909, 1919, and 1933) and later of the Ministry of Education (*Moving and Growing* and *Planning the Programme*, 1947) make clear the trends towards greater freedom for the individual and less formality, features which have characterised the changes in the lesson since the beginning of this century. The drill lesson, with its military precision, was succeeded by the physical training lesson with its recreative activities, vaulting and agility practices, relay races and breaks, but with emphasis on exercises based on the Swedish system of physical education.

Successful progress is usually a gradual process and worthwhile changes emerge from and are built upon the better aspects of previous work. Change for its own sake is not necessarily beneficial; all that was done previously was not necessarily bad and all that is new is not of necessity good. There is no real advantage to be gained by changing something that has proved successful and even when making comparatively drastic changes in the presentation of their work, teachers have been wise to retain those aspects which they have found to be successful and of real value.

It is perhaps of interest to outline some of the factors which influenced the writers of this book towards a consideration of ways in which the teaching of gymnastics should develop. It is perhaps not generally realised that signs of dissatisfaction with some aspects of the traditional approach and with some of the actual material content of the lesson itself were already being manifested during the 1930s. This dissatisfaction was prompted by a desire for greater flexibility and freedom in the lesson and for a reduction in the degree of formality and regimentation. It was also evident that there was a desire and even a need to replace artificial exercises, which had so strong a bias towards corrective and remedial effects, with activities of a more active, natural and dynamic character. This was our own experience, an experience which was shared by many others.

It was recognised that real achievement in vaulting and agility activities was the province of the few and that success enjoyed by the gifted performers was not shared by all. The appeal inherent in the type of work being done was limited to those with natural ability and it became obvious that a radical change of approach would be necessary before any noteworthy improvement on a class basis could be effected. The war-time experiences of many physical education specialists who served in the various branches of the armed forces tended to support this view. The introduction of more purposeful activities into the fitness training schedules of service personnel represented a revolutionary change of approach. Exercises performed in lines and in unison to an instructor's word of command were largely replaced by more interesting and objective practices performed with logs, sticks, medicine balls, and so on. Recreative activities of various kinds, performed individually, with partners or in small groups, proved both effective and popular, and the later introduction of climbing units, obstacle courses, horizontal, oblique and vertical rope traverses, often constituting 'man-size' jungle-gyms, indicated a distinct trend of the future. The need to devise practices and effective techniques for lifting and carrying heavy objects and for jumping on to or from moving vehicles proved a most worthwhile challenge. This together with the urgent need to discover solutions to the hazards associated with parachute landings presented situations which demanded thought, inventiveness and improvisation on the part of both instructor and pupil. This seems to indicate a clear link with, if not the foundation for, many ideas which have been accepted as successful features of post-war work in schools.

Experimentation with different teaching techniques, the elimination of formal exercises and commands, the discarding of static formations and positions, the greater use of apparatus and the introduction of a greater variety of both small and large equipment were significant aspects of the immediate post-war changes. This new approach to teaching made its greatest initial impact in infant and junior schools and in some areas, notably Halifax, much successful work was done, and films made in 1948 to illustrate the work attracted much attention and made a great impact throughout the country. Without doubt the ideas prevalent at that time had a great effect on future developments and the more general acceptance by teachers of the need to cater for the individuality of children led to a greater use of opportunities for free practice and to the introduction of opportunities for free choice, experimentation, exploration and the exercise of the imagination.

Similar significant developments were taking place in the field of dance, influenced by and based upon the Laban theories and principles of movement. Though these developments were operating within a different aspect of physical activity, there were distinct similarities in the teaching methods being used and the developments taking place in the field of gymnastics largely because each endeavoured to cater for the individuality of children and to provide opportunities for creative work. Teaching methods in dance and gymnastics have developed on almost identical lines and while the movement qualities of time, weight, space and flow which are such prominent features of the Laban philosophy have become important influences on the development of a modern approach to the teaching of gymnastics, the more objective characteristics of gymnastics have influenced the teaching of creative dance.

Early experimentation on a new approach to teaching, influenced by the several factors mentioned, enjoyed considerable success during the early post-war period. The enthusiasm engendered in both teachers and children in the primary schools was very evident. The reaction and response of the children were a revelation, and so different was the attitude to the work that one felt that a new subject had been introduced into the curriculum. This enthusiasm was reflected in the attitude of the teachers. They readily appreciated the close relationship between the methods and techniques employed and those used by them in the classroom. They also appreciated the close link between these developments and the general trends in educational thought towards the realisation of the need to cater for the individual. The favourable comments made by inspectors, headteachers, parents, school medical officers and others closely concerned with education provided tremendous encouragement and it soon became apparent to those also engaged in and concerned with secondary work that it was necessary to adopt similar ideas and to introduce work based on the same principles for older children.

The difference between a primary school child and a secondary school boy or girl, chronologically, is only about six weeks and even though they are placed in a different environment it seems quite inappropriate for the methods by which they are taught to differ radically. Experimentation with those ideas which had proved so successful in the primary school met with equal success at the secondary level and gradually a similar pattern of development began to unfold. Specialist teachers, whose training had been on formal and traditional lines, were naturally somewhat slow to change their methods, but the standards of work produced, the enthusiasm, enjoyment and obvious satisfaction of both pupils and teachers, the ideas created, the amount of work being done and the achievements experienced by all rather than the few, began to have their effect, and great interest in the development of secondary work was stimulated. Much critical appraisal of the work done and the methods being employed was to be expected, but once a start was made progress was encouraging. The interest, reaction and enthusiasm of secondary school pupils, at all levels, have compared favourably with the attitude and response experienced with younger children and it was clear that the appeal of this approach was not limited to any particular age group. Outstanding success has been achieved in all types of schools not only at the primary level and at the lower end of the secondary school but also with older pupils and with students in colleges of education.

There seems no limit to the ways in which this work can develop. New ideas and new facets emerge daily and this adds to the interest, satisfaction and enthusiasm of both teacher and pupils. The desire for help in implementing this type of work is evidenced by the tremendous demand for and attendances at teachers' courses conducted by local education authorities and national associations in all parts of the country and in many parts of the world.

To distinguish the modern approach from the more formal traditional teaching methods employed, it has become common practice to refer to this aspect of physical education as *educational gymnastics*. This, it is felt, has been particularly valuable during the period when the basic principles underlying this new approach to the teaching of gymnastics were being developed and established and their practical application implemented. The term, however, has often been the subject of criticism by those who have asked: 'why educational gymnastics and not educational English, educational mathematics or educational art?' Why indeed? The use of the term can be justified from at least two points of view:

a   It has discriminated between the new teaching methods used and the traditional approach previously employed and has emphasised during a period of transition the need to realise that teaching methods have undergone radical changes.

b   It is the presentation of gymnastics based on sound educational principles.

The principles underlying the work, the methods of presentation employed and the teaching techniques used are now so well established that no doubt the time will come when it will no longer be necessary to use the term educational gymnastics. If this happens it will be possible to return to the use of the term gymnastics because it will apply to the gymnastics lesson as it is known today and not to the traditional lesson of what might be called the pre-educational gymnastics era.

It has been an exciting experience to take an active part in the development of the modern approach to the teaching of gymnastics, to be privileged to work with the children and to give help and guidance to many teachers in all types of schools. There is no doubt that the changes made in the teaching of gymnastics have been amongst the most important trends in the development of physical education during the last twenty years or more.

In view of this contention it may be appropriate and relevant to discuss briefly some of the more significant features of the revolutionary changes that have taken place in the realm of gymnastics. Our aim in doing this is to help teachers to appreciate the main differences between the old and the new methods of teaching and to hope that the information given might help them to estimate whether their own work measures up to modern requirements and how far they have travelled along the road of new ideas. Our previous book *Physical Education in the Primary School* refers to these characteristics of modern work and it is hoped to discuss them even more fully in a future publication.

21 Features of modern work in gymnastics

a An individual approach

Perhaps the most important feature of modern work in gymnastics is the way in which children are dealt with as individuals who vary in physique, physical ability and attitude and that teachers now cater for each individual within the class rather than for the class unit. This individual approach implies not only that each child responds in his own individual way but also that the teacher recognises the individual differences in children and expects each child to respond individually and therefore differently in most situations. The teacher, moreover, not only accepts the fact that these individual differences exist, but he modifies his approach, his method and his teaching technique to accommodate each individual within the class as far as is humanly possible. This is a challenge to all teachers, but the reward and satisfaction are reflected in the success and the sense of personal achievement enjoyed by both child and teacher.

There is an additional point. Not only do the children benefit from this individual approach, but so does the teacher, for the many ideas which emerge from the opportunities for individual experimentation enrich his, as well as their, conception of the scope and content of gymnastics. All the methods, techniques, features and principles involved in this approach to teaching are geared to the demand, the necessity and the purpose of accommodating each individual child irrespective of attitude, aptitude and ability.

b Natural activities and movements

Adult-imposed exercises such as arms bending and stretching have been discarded and the content of the work is based on natural activities. Running, jumping, climbing, rolling, balancing, swinging, heaving and other natural activities and movements form the foundation upon which the work is built. Activities and movements are referred to rather than exercises and those activities or movements which end in *ing* form an excellent basis for successful work. Subsidiary considerations such as speed, direction, shape, and so on become influencing factors related to the main task of *doing* or *moving*.

c Analysis of movement

The work is now considered more in terms of the efficiency of the body as a whole than in terms of the strength, mobility, or suppleness of particular parts of the body. Previously, exercises were analysed anatomically in terms of the muscle groups being used (abdominal, lateral, dorsal, etc.), the joints involved (hips, shoulders, etc.), and the physical effects (strength, mobility, endurance, etc.). Exercises for isolated muscle groups were devised accordingly. A different and in some ways a more comprehensive analysis is now used:
    i) the *type of movement* being performed – rolling, stretching, twisting, balancing, etc.;
    ii) the *body part or parts* being used – arms, legs, etc.;
    iii) the *part of the body on* which the movement is being performed – hands, back, shoulders, etc.;
    iv) the *space* factor and how the body is being used in relation to the space available – high, low, in the air, on the move, inverted, etc.;
    v) the *shape* of the body – long, wide, symmetrical, etc.;
    vi) the *speed* of the movement – quick, slow, very quick, etc.;
    vii) the *direction* in which the body moves – forwards, upwards, backwards, etc.;
    viii) the *prepositional relationship* of the body to the apparatus being used – over, through, off, along, etc.;

ix) the *management of body weight* factor – supporting, propelling, absorbing, transferring, etc.

To many teachers this analysis will be new and perhaps somewhat revolutionary, and it might help to give an illustration of its application with reference to a familiar, popular and traditional gymnastic activity – handstanding. A handstand is a balance on the hands, but it will be seen from the following summary that this activity could be analysed in several different ways.

A HANDSTAND IS—
- —a balance,
- —a stretched position,
- —an inverted position,
- —a symmetrical shape,
- —a long and narrow shape,
- —a position where the body weight is supported on the hands,
- —a balance on hands
- —an inverted position on the hands,
- —a symmetrical balance,
- —a position where the feet are the highest part,
- —a stretched movement on the hands,
- —a symmetrical balance on the hands.

If this type of analysis is used, the teacher provides himself with an extensive repertoire of tasks, any of which could be developed in many ways. Such developments are not possible if the activity is regarded merely as a teacher-imposed skill, complete in itself. For example, if handstanding has been practised as a form of balance on the hands, the teacher could lead the children into experimental work on:

- —other kinds of balance,
- —other kinds of balance on the hands,
- —other ways of inverting the body,
- —other ways of stretching,
- —other kinds of shapes on the hands,
- —other ways of moving on the hands, etc.

It will be seen that the possibilities for development are considerable and that this method of analysis constitutes an important, valuable and productive feature of this approach.

d   The scope and content of gymnastics

An analysis of movements and activities as outlined in Section (c) leads to a wide and rich conception of the content of the work, and it will be appreciated that ideas for implementation and development with all these considerations in mind are unlimited. Thus, the interpretation of what is meant by gymnastics has altered considerably. The scope of the work, which is now accepted, not only includes the traditional vaulting and agility activities, but also the unlimited number of movements and patterns of movements which result from using varied methods of presentation in a variety of physical situations which allow opportunities for invention, and exploration. Gymnastics, no less than art, music, drama, becomes a subject for unending experimentation and for the exercise of imagination and the development of creative ability.

e   Informality

There has been much misunderstanding and indeed misuse of the words *formal*, *informal* and *free* in relation to the new approach to the teaching of gymnastics. Informality is a salient feature of modern teaching, but the need for teachers to be prepared to resort to a degree of formality as and when the occasion demands must be recognised. The absence of artificial and unnatural regimentation, the elimination of the unnecessary use of formations such as circles or straight lines, the freer use of space, and a less rigid, less formal atmosphere throughout the lesson, have combined to produce a more natural class–teacher relationship in which the natural learning processes can be exercised with greater effect. There are some teachers who consider that informality of necessity results in a lack or a loss of discipline, but it has been found that the reverse is true. Good discipline is self-discipline and is a natural result of purposeful activity in which each child develops the ability to cope adequately and confidently in the various situations in which he finds himself. It is wrong to consider that a teacher must belong to either the formal or the informal category – all teachers should be prepared, if necessary, to be formal one moment and informal the next.

Free practice

The opportunities given for children to practise on their own, in their own time, form another aspect of the informality of a modern lesson. This free practice has replaced the class controlled exercises which were performed to a class rhythm imposed by the teacher. There was, however, some satisfaction and enjoyment derived from working in unison, but in many instances class unison assumed a much greater importance than the standard of performance of the exercises themselves. The satisfaction and pleasure experienced in moving together can still be enjoyed when teachers provide opportunities for partner and group cooperation. 'Matching' and 'mirror' work by partners or groups emphasise this point and show how the more valuable features of previous work are being used effectively and realistically to enrich the work of the present.

g Free choice

This must not be confused with 'free practice'. A salient feature of modern gymnastics is the opportunity given for children to choose for themselves. Sometimes they are free to choose, to experiment, to devise within the limitation of a given task, while on other occasions they might be completely free to work within the limitations of the space available or the equipment being used.

Those classes which have been taught specific activities by traditional methods would derive much benefit from opportunities to choose freely from the activities they have been taught. This would reflect the effectiveness of their training and give their work a new dimension. Choice is related to past experience and ability and may need to be guided within the bounds of good sense and reason. Development of the ability to choose wisely and sensibly is perhaps one of the most important features, not only of gymnastics but of the whole of a modern physical education programme. Children must become accustomed to freedom; they must be able in due course to be trusted to choose with care and discretion and to accept the responsibilities which this implies. Surely this is a basic feature not only of physical education but of education and of life.

h Conversational teaching

One of the most striking features of modern work is the replacement of the drill technique of the instructor by a more natural conversational manner similar to that adopted in the classroom when dealing with other subjects. Formal commanding, for so long regarded as an important factor in the teaching of gymnastics, involved the use of an agreed pattern consisting of an explanatory part, a pause and an executive word of command:

'On the feet . . . up!'

'To the wall bars . . . run!'

'Trunk slowly . . . unroll!'

'Skip jumping with arms bending and stretching forwards, upwards and sideways, finishing in a crouch position on the 8th count . . . begin!'

These examples serve to remind us of the amount of time which was involved in learning how to command correctly and effectively. Students in training spent many sessions with partners or in small groups taking part in commanding practice and endeavouring to perfect their ability to indicate the type of movement to be done, by appropriate voice inflexion and by varying the length of the pause. The ability to teach well was very closely linked with the ability to command effectively.

It is now realised that though there might be times when a forceful command may be necessary or advantageous, a more conversational teaching manner is much more natural and effective. The teacher's real contribution is made after the class has begun to work, by stimulation and coaching. A conversational manner, however, should not be confused with quiet teaching completely lacking in drive or stimulation. The more effective teachers, though normally quiet and persuasive, find it necessary at times to be forceful, aggressive and demanding.

i Experimentation and exploration

The opportunities afforded children to explore and to experiment within the situations presented, or the tasks imposed, constitute an important feature of modern gymnastics. In the teaching and presentation of any subject, whether practical or academic, methods which stimulate the use of the imagination and which encourage the development of creative ability and powers of inventiveness, together with opportunities to develop still further on the results of such exploration, have important educational implications. These implications have been appreciated and fully recognised by educationists in general during the development of modern ideas in the teaching of gymnastics.

j Methods of presentation

In recent years the most significant change in the approach to the teaching of gymnastics, and the one which embodies all other features of the work, is the fact that three methods of presentation are now employed. In the traditional approach to the teaching of gymnastics only one method, the *direct* method of presentation, was used, a particular exercise or movement, vault or agility being imposed on the class by the teacher. Now three methods are used:

i) the *direct* method of presentation, in which the teacher imposes a specific activity,

ii) the *indirect* method of presentation, where the children are completely free to choose or devise their own activities or movements within the limits of the space and apparatus at their disposal,

iii) the *limitation* method of presentation, when the children are allowed to choose freely within the limitations imposed by the teacher. The limitation is the task or challenge imposed.

It is only by making appropriate use of these three methods of presentation, either singly or in combination, both with and without apparatus, on an individual, partner and group basis that the best results are obtained and that the many features referred to in this section become possible. It is only in this way, for example, that progression on an individual basis can be satisfactorily developed, that opportunities for experimentation and exploration can be provided, that creative ability and inventiveness can be encouraged, and that the educational and democratic values of individual choice can be exploited. The success of this modern approach depends on a thorough understanding of all that is involved in the practical application of these three methods of presentation.

k The lesson plan

Teachers require a lesson plan or framework for their lesson to ensure that a sensible balance is kept between the various aspects or phases of the work. There is much to commend the theory of harmonious development and it is still necessary, not only to ensure that all parts of the body are used and that skill and ability on as wide a scale as possible are developed, but also that the situations in which the children are placed and the tasks set will provide them with the broadest and richest experience possible.

The simplified lesson plan, which is a feature of modern work, enables teachers to give more comprehensive attention to the aspects or phases of which the lesson is composed and indicates clearly that in the second part of the lesson a generous amount of time should be allocated to group work using large apparatus. The changes made in respect of the lesson plan are indicated in Figs 20, 21 and 22 on pages 85 and 86. They show details of old plans which many teachers will remember and a typical new plan. Without going into more detail at this stage it will be seen that the new lesson plan suggested in Fig. 22 is very different in its structure from previous lesson plans and reflects the very different conception of the work.

PART ONE
Introductory excercise
Rhythmic jump
Head and neck or trunk bend. D
Arm and shoulder
Trunk bending or turning sideways
Leg and balance
PART TWO
Class activity
Group practices
Game and final exercise

FIGURE 20 (ABOVE) *A typical 1933 syllabus lesson plan (primary schools)*

FIGURE 21 (RIGHT) *A typical reference book lesson plan (secondary schools)*

PART ONE–SECTION ONE
Introductory activity
Rhythmic jump
Dorsal
Arm and shoulder
Leg and balance
Lateral
Abdominal
PART ONE–SECTION TWO
Dorsal
Complimentary abdominal
Lateral
Leg and balance
PART TWO
Class activity
Group activities
Final exercise (depletive)

PART ONE		PART TWO
The introductory phase		The group work phase
The running–jumping and landing phase		
The teacher selects and deals with one or two of these phases	The balance phase	
	The body movement phase	
	The weight on hands phase	
	The class activity phase	

FIGURE 22 *A typical lesson plan of today – primary or secondary schools*

1 Group work

The second part of the lesson consists of group activities involving the use of large portable and fixed apparatus. Since the first part of the lesson is shorter than in previous lesson plans (compare Figs 21 and 22), a more generous amount of time can be given to the group work phase in which much that has been learnt in part 1 of the lesson can be applied to the large apparatus situations. A feature of modern work, therefore, is the much greater prominence and importance given to this part of the lesson.

Because of the increased amount of time allocated to group work, because of the use of the three methods of presentation applied singly or in combination, because of the considerably greater use of large apparatus, and because of the very close relationship with the work done in part 1 of the lesson, group work has become very much more active, interesting, challenging and demanding. Standards of performance, relative to each child's innate ability, have vastly improved and the many ideas evolved, the various ways in which the apparatus is used, and the interesting and exciting individual, partner and group sequences developed, have combined to provide work of a quality and variety which have exceeded the most optimistic hopes. Another feature of group work is the number and size of the groups. Groups usually consist of four or five pupils, certainly not more than six, so that each child is involved actively for most of the time, allowing greatly increased opportunities for practice and repetition. Working continuously is an outstanding feature and waiting for turns is unnecessary. Figures 23 and 24 (pages 88 and 90–1) compare a typical traditional arrangement of apparatus for group work and an example of group apparatus as it would be used today.

m Range of equipment

Another interesting development of recent years, at both primary and secondary level, has been the introduction of new types of apparatus. In planning new facilities there is an attempt to include different types of equipment because each creates a different situation and thereby prompts different ideas, giving children a richer experience. Such new equipment includes the trampette and the trampoline and many types of ingeniously designed climbing and heaving units. Several types of equipment, such as rings, window ladders, rope-ladders, the trapeze, vertical, oblique and horizontal climbing bars and ropes, which for a long time have been out of favour, have been restored to useful service. All these, together with the more familiar items of equipment such as benches, beams, wall bars, vaulting boxes, vaulting horses, rubber landing and agility mats, and so on, present the teacher with opportunities for creating a greater variety of challenging and demanding situations.

n Combining apparatus

One of the most significant features of a modern interpretation of group work is the fact that whereas in the past, in most instances, one major piece of apparatus only was used (see Fig. 25, page 92), several pieces of apparatus are now used in combination. Such combinations, an example of which is shown in Fig. 26 (page 93), present new and challenging situations which prompt a tremendous variety of ideas. The pupils are stimulated to evolve their own sequences or patterns of movement using in their own way the items of equipment available to them and this makes the work far more demanding and interesting and enables the children to enjoy much richer gymnastic experiences.

o Relationship of part 1 of the lesson to part 2

Previously, part 1 of the lesson consisted of exercises based on Scandinavian theories and principles, aimed primarily to promote strength of muscle groups and mobility of joints and often performed

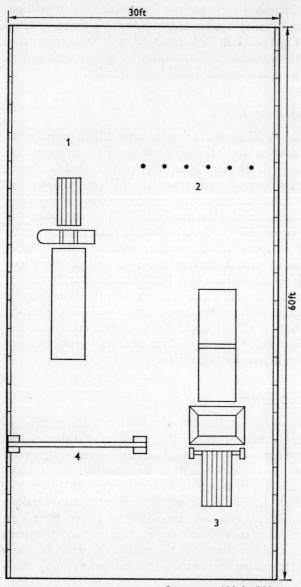

Gymnasium 60ft by 30ft

Group 1 – Beating board, vaulting horse, agility mat
Group 2 – Six climbing ropes
Group 3 – Springboard, vaulting box, two 6ft by 4ft mats
Group 4 – Beam (e.g. hole 21)

FIGURE 23 *Group work in gymnastics – a traditiona arrangement of apparatus*

for their corrective and remedial value. It is generally agreed that there was little direct relationship between part 1 and the vaulting and agility practices of part 2 of the lesson. As already stated, the exercises have now been replaced in part 1 by activities and movements such as rolling, stretching, balancing, supporting the body weight in different ways, jumping, twisting, and so on, and the experiences gained and the skill developed are applied to the different apparatus situations of part 2. The confidence evident in group work is a direct result of the experience, coaching and practice enjoyed in the earlier phases of the lesson.

p Coaching

A distinguishing feature of a modern lesson in gymnastics is the amount and variety of coaching done by the teacher. Though the basic techniques of teaching remain the same, irrespective of the subject, in gymnastics coaching has replaced correction and the subtle and skilful use of different coaching methods combine to produce much more effective and rewarding teaching. Great similarity can be seen with the methods and teaching techniques used in the classroom, where the teacher's powers of stimulation, inspiration, suggestion, encouragement, help and guidance are supplemented by the use of demonstration and observation and the employment of the question and answer technique. These various aspects of successful coaching form the basis of effective teaching. Without them standards of work remain inferior and teaching becomes a most unrewarding experience.

q Sequence work

Another very important and attractive feature of current methods in gymnastics is the attention given to sequence work of all types, with and without apparatus. In the past, sequence work was normally restricted to the talented few and the sequences were usually teacher imposed. In modern work each individual is given opportunities to devise his own sequences and as a result sequence work becomes the province of all, rather than the few.

The enjoyment and satisfaction associated with sequence work, either individually, in pairs, or in groups, is very apparent, and there is no doubt that this has become one of the most successful and popular features of modern work.

FIGURE 24 *Group work in gymnastics – a typical arrangement of apparatus today*

Group 1 Inclined bench on lower beam, beam saddle above on upper beam, two mats, beating board, climbing ropes and adjacent wallbars

Group 2 Bench, agility mat, vaulting horse

Group 3 Two beams at different heights, inclined bench to wallbars, beam saddle on lower beam, bench under lower beam (also used by Group 4)

Group 4 Trampette, three mats, springboard, vaulting box, adjacent wallbars (also bench used by Group 3)

Group 5 Two sets of window ladders

Group 6 Inclined bench on lower beam at box height, inclined bench to top beam, beam saddle, vaulting box, one mat, adjacent wallbars, climbing ropes (also used by Group 7)

Group 7 Inverted beam, inclined bench on wallbars, one mat (also climbing ropes used by Group 6)

Group 8 Bench, trampette, vaulting buck, agility mat, adjacent wallbars, one mat

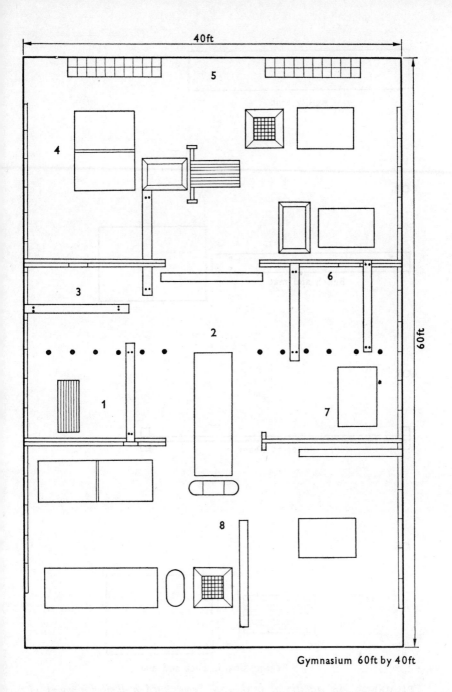

40ft

5

4

3

2

1

6

7

8

60ft

Gymnasium 60ft by 40ft

91

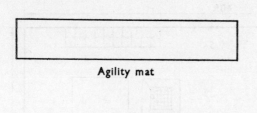

Agility mat

OR

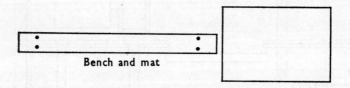

Bench and mat

OR

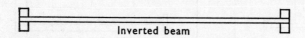

Inverted beam

OR

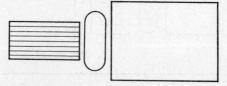

Beating board, buck and mat

FIGURE 25 *In traditional work each group used a limited amount of apparatus*

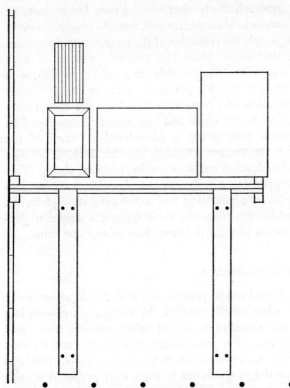

Climbing ropes, inclined benches on lower beam at box
height, vaulting box, beating board, two mats, adjacent
wallbars and surrounding floor area

FIGURE 26 *In modern work each group is allocated several items of
apparatus in combination*

r Progression and development

Progression and standards of work are no longer judged in relation to
the difficulty of the exercises given to different age groups. Many
teachers will remember that exercises were made more difficult for
older children by various means, such as reducing the base of support, changing the position of the arms, or by performing exercises
with different parts of the body at the same time to make coordination
more difficult. In vaulting and agility the normal teaching pattern
consisted of a series of progressive stages leading from elementary to
more advanced work. These progressive stages were applied to the
class as a whole so that some children were not extended, while the
demands made on others were in excess of their capabilities.

In a modern approach the teacher realises that development or progress is entirely an individual matter and that the improvement of the class as a whole is only the reflection of the progress made by each individual within that class. Since the rate of progress of each individual varies, it is virtually impossible for a teacher to plan, with certainty, for the class to reach a particular stage at any particular time. This interpretation of progression based on the class rather than on the individual is unreliable and educationally unacceptable.

In modern work, progression is considered in terms of the opportunities which the teacher provides and the methods he uses for each individual to develop and improve his physical ability. This implies not only improvement in the quality of performance but also a greater capacity for implementing and developing new ideas, for using initiative and imagination, and for acquiring a deeper understanding and awareness of what is being done at any one time.

s   Chronological considerations

Closely related to the subject of progression and development is the age factor in the selection of material. In the past, free-standing exercises and the traditional vaulting and agility activities prescribed for any class were part of a programme of work devised for that particular age group. An examination of pre-war textbooks confirms this and shows how the programmes of work were prepared in such a way that they increased in difficulty according to the age of the class. Age, however, is not a reliable guide to physical ability and the content of each lesson is now related to the ability of the individual members within it. Classes do not make progress at similar rates. Children in one class, because of a wealth of natural talent, will progress much more rapidly than those of an older but less gifted age group, and teachers frequently find themselves imposing more difficult tasks and presenting more difficult situations for a younger class because of the natural ability of the children in it. It is necessary for teachers to realise that any class is as good as he or she can make it, but that, on the other hand, it will only be as good as the natural ability, aptitude and attitude of its members will allow – thoughts which constitute both a challenge and a consolation.

t   Class teacher relationship

The most significant feature of all, perhaps the sum total of all the features of modern work, is the change in class–teacher relationship – the establishment of which is a first requirement of effective and successful teaching. Class–teacher relationship has undoubtedly improved and learning has become a more enjoyable experience because of the following factors:

    i) the child is now allowed to develop as an individual;
    ii) frequent opportunities are provided for exercising choice;
    iii) the teacher recognises individual problems and that progress is an individual matter;
    iv) stimulation and encouragement are more frequently given;
    v) coaching methods are more varied and effective;
    vi) there is an informal and pleasant atmosphere of purposeful endeavour;
    vii) a sense of achievement is more often experienced by each child;
    viii) each pupil copes adequately with the situations in which he is placed;
    ix) each child enjoys a sense of adequacy and security;
    x) each child is purposefully and actively employed;
    xi) teachers are less detached and are more approachable.

This improved relationship between teacher and class has been most frequently commented upon by those teachers who have had considerable experience of both traditional and modern methods and by others concerned with the more academic aspects of education who have had opportunities to observe physical education based on modern ideas.

Having referred to the more salient features associated with a modern approach to the teaching of gymnastics and having discussed some of the principles on which the changes are based, it is hoped, in a subsequent publication, to give an indication of the ways in which the ideas expressed can be successfully implemented. Successful implementation, however, can only result if understanding and conviction are linked with enthusiasm, knowledge and sound teaching ability.

22 Final comments

In Part One of this book the major trends and developments in physical education in the post-war years have been discussed. Amongst other things, the basic philosophy underlying modern physical education, the principles involved, the methods used and the expansion in the scope and content of the programme have been considered. The success which has accompanied these developments is reflected in the words of a former Minister of Education who, speaking at an International Conference on Physical Education, said:

> 'In no field of Education have there been such radical changes in purpose and content as in the field of Physical Education. Physical Education is an essential part of general Education and the first class teacher of Physical Education is no less important than the first class teacher of any other subject.'

These developments should not only be of vital interest and concern to all teachers of physical education, but they should prompt the question each should ask – 'Am I keeping pace with modern trends and developments and does my work reflect the changes which have taken place?' There is no doubt that experimentation by teachers and pupils will continue, leading to further changes in the content of the subject and the methods of implementation. It is to be hoped that those aspects of the physical education programme which have special educational value will continue to find a prominent place and that teachers will adopt a sympathetic and progressive attitude towards change. To stand still is to stagnate and stagnation is the enemy of progress.

Tudor Powell Jones, now vice-principal of a college of education, writes: 'Education is the main force moulding the society of the future. It is desirable therefore that it should be using the methods of the present day.' And Sir Ronald Gould at a recent conference said, 'Teachers must respond to the need for change.' It must be accepted that change is inevitable in a progressive society; it is equally inevitable in progressive education and in progressive physical education. Teachers must be selective and must ensure that any change made in their approach to their work is a change, not just for its own sake, but in their view a change for the better and for the benefit of those whom they teach.

Useful publications (see page 60)

Planning for Sport (The Sports Council, 26 Park Crescent, London, W1N 4AJ)
Halls for Badminton (Badminton Association of England, 81a High Street, Bromley, Kent)
Community Sports Halls (a report of the Research Fellowship set up jointly by the National Playing Fields Association of 57B Catherine Place, London, SW1 and the Central Council of Physical Recreation)

Part Two

Planning the physical education programme

1 The expanding curriculum

Section 7 in Part One (see pages 23–5) of this book makes reference to the great expansion in the scope and content of the physical education programme in schools during the last twenty years. This widening or expansion of the curriculum brings with it many accompanying problems, the solutions to which demand considerable thought and indicate the need for careful selection in the planning of a school's programme. The wide nature of the curriculum as illustrated in Fig. 3 ('Physical education today'), page 24, indicates that the programme now includes some or all of the following:

Athletics   *a* Field events
              b Track events
              c Training schedules, including weight training, circuit training, interval training, etc.

Cross-country running

Educational gymnastics

Major games   *a* Association football
              b Rugby football
              c Hockey
              d Lacrosse
              e Netball
              f Cricket
              g Tennis
              h Golf
              i Volleyball
              j Rounders
              k Basketball
              l Badminton

Minor games and games practices

Dance	*a* National and folk dancing
	b Modern and old-time ballroom dancing
	c Creative dance
Swimming	*a* Basic strokes
	b Diving
	c Life-saving and resuscitation
	d Survival swimming
	e Sub-aqua activities

Outdoor Activities

    a Archery
    b Camping, including mobile camping
    c Canoeing
    d Fell-walking
    e Mountaineering
    f Rock-climbing
    g Orienteering
    h Sailing
    i Duke of Edinburgh Award Scheme

Indoor Activities

    a Fencing
    b Judo
    c Rebound tumbling
    d Table-tennis
    e Squash

2 The general problems

The time allocated to physical education has not increased pro-
portionately to the increased breadth of the subject and this constitutes the main problem that each teacher has to solve for himself.
He must decide not only which aspects or activities to include in his
scheme but also the amount of time which can justifiably and satisfactorily be allocated to each. The real danger is that the programme
can easily become a mile wide but only an inch deep, a criticism that
is in many instances justified. In attempting to include everything, or
nearly everything, invariably nothing is done well. Variety for its
own sake is not necessarily a good thing. Indeed, a justifiable criticism
of many teachers is that, although they present a varied programme,

no worthwhile standards are achieved in anything and neither the children nor the teachers experience a real sense of satisfaction. By presenting so wide and varied a programme, depth and quality are sacrificed for width and variety, and this lack of quality is often due to inadequate planning and preparation and to an insufficient allocation of time to any one aspect of the work to permit satisfactory progress to high standards.

The developing of worthwhile standards of work requires great effort and perseverance, and when planning a programme the problem for each teacher is concerned not only with methods of presentation, but also with the time factor and the sensible selection of activities from those that are possible. No teacher is expected to be an expert in all facets of physical education and teachers are wise to ensure that they include in their programme those aspects of which they have special knowledge and experience. If facilities and time are available to permit the inclusion of other activities in which they are not expert, they themselves should endeavour to seek further knowledge and training and in addition should enlist the help and support of other members of staff who are able to make their own special contributions. In this way more aspects can satisfactorily be made available to the pupils.

It is appropriate to be reminded that one of the most significant features of post-war developments in both academic and practical subjects has been that teaching methods have been modified in order to cater for the individual differences and varying abilities and interests of each pupil. Of equal importance is the fact that each teacher is also an individual who is not only entitled to his own point of view, but is also entitled to deal with his subject in his own particular way, both in relation to the content of his syllabus and the approach or method he adopts in the presentation of any one aspect of it. But each teacher should be able to justify his programme and his methods to himself and to others, not only in terms of the principles underlying his work but also in terms of the results obtained and the standards achieved. When, for example, a teacher includes athletics in his programme and teaches it in a particular way which may perhaps be regarded as unorthodox, he should be able to explain his reasons for this and to justify his ideas and methods in terms of the principles involved and the results achieved. If he can do this, no one should deny him the privilege of teaching his subject in his way.

There are many values which accrue from the introduction into the physical education programme of coaching in the major team games, of swimming, badminton, athletics, outdoor pursuits and all the other activities already mentioned. All are worthy of a place in the programme of physical education. But the needs of a class and in particular the needs of every individual within that class must be carefully considered. When the limited amount of time available and the frequent limitations of facilities are also considered, the inevitable problem to be solved is that of planning a curriculum which will best meet the many and varied requirements of each individual. A lesson in any aspect of physical education must be assessed physically and educationally and we should ask ourselves, not only whether each pupil has been extended physically in as all-embracing a way as possible but also whether he has been sufficiently challenged mentally. Not only should he have improved physically in terms of fitness and physical ability, but he should also have been given opportunities for exercising initiative and inventiveness and for expressing some degree of choice. Irrespective of the activity being taught, due consideration must be given to the fact that each child is an individual who varies not only in physique and physical ability, but also in attitude. There is no doubt that the more this principle of dealing with pupils as individuals is adopted and applied, the more successful will the teacher be, whether he is dealing with gymnastics, swimming, or any other particular activity on the one hand, or with optional activities on the other. Physical education lessons, both in content and method, have been modified to meet the needs of individuals and this has resulted in developments which can confidently be described as rich and rewarding, giving intense satisfaction to both teachers and pupils. But to be fully effective, the lessons must be carefully planned and prepared.

3 The three levels of planning

The vital necessity for careful planning of the programme as a whole has been stressed as a pre-requisite of any successful work. It would appear that such planning must be concerned with three levels or depths of preparation, each of which require careful consideration. These levels are concerned with:

a   the preparation of the over-all programme or curriculum for the complete age range of the school;

b   the preparation of the more detailed schemes of work for each individual aspect of the over-all programme referred to in (a); and

c   the even more detailed day-to-day preparation of lessons for the implementation and development of the individual aspects of the programme referred to in (b).

The preparation required therefore covers *a) programme or curriculum; b) schemes of work; c) lessons.*

4   The values of preparation

In every teaching situation there would appear to be three distinct phases: *a) preparation and planning; b) implementation; c) reflection and recording.*

These three phases apply equally to the planning of the programme as a whole, to the preparation of a scheme of work and to the detailed requirements of any one lesson. Although it is intended to refer to the problems of implementation and the values of reflection and recording later in the book, the specific aim of Part Two is to discuss the first of the three phases referred to above – the preparation and planning stage, in particular as it relates to the school's physical education programme as a whole.

What are the real advantages to be gained from careful planning and preparation?

a   Immediately the teacher applies himself to the process of preparation, thought is given to the task in hand and a conscientious attitude is thereby indicated and developed. This in itself is of great value and implies a systematic, thoughtful and calculating approach to teaching.

b   Effective preparation should ensure:
i) that an intelligent appraisal has been made of all the factors, human and material, which influence the production of successful work and to which detailed reference will be made later;
ii) that the basic philosophy on which the aims and objectives of the work are based is satisfied.

c   Careful preparation should guarantee a balanced and well-blended programme of work. The increased width of the programme has accentuated the problem of balance and blend and has emphasised the need for more careful planning than was required when the scope of the curriculum was so very much more limited.

d   Preparation of a programme, a scheme of work, or a single lesson automatically provides a record of what, it is hoped, will be done. Such information, when later examined and suitably modified in the light of actual experience, provides a record of what has been accomplished and becomes an invaluable basis for future planning of the work.

e   When planning for the future, reference to the records of work done allows the teacher to make comparisons between the programmes or lessons for different classes and age groups at any time during the year and between similar classes and age groups in different years.

f   Planning is essential in order to provide a carefully graduated programme for the different age groups to which it applies, so that the teacher-selected programme of the early years of the secondary school can gradually develop into a more appropriate programme for older pupils, where individual choice and option can be exercised.

g   Perhaps more important than the effects of careful preparation on the programme itself are the personal and psychological values for the teacher in the practical and realistic lesson situation. When sound preparation of the over-all programme and of the schemes of work has been supplemented by careful planning for the immediate requirements of a particular lesson, there are many distinct personal and psychological advantages for the teacher; for example:

i) The teacher is more confident because he knows what he intends to teach – a vital factor in successful teaching.

ii) Because he knows what he intends to teach, the teacher is able to concentrate more on what he *is doing* rather than on wondering what he *is going to do.*

iii) Knowing clearly what he is doing, the teacher is able to concentrate much more on *how* he is teaching rather than on *what* he is teaching. This enables him to think more about his teaching technique and how skilfully and appropriately he uses the invaluable coaching methods of demonstration, observation and stimulation – so essential in successful teaching situations.

iv) As a result of these factors, standards of teaching improve immeasurably.

What further evidence is required than this, to justify the need for careful and adequate preparation? All teachers are capable of sound preparation even if they are not all equally gifted in their powers of implementation, but none can afford to neglect the obvious help which planning will give. It is well to remember that '*teaching begins where organisation ends*' and that the total teaching situation involves all three of the phases already referred to, i.e. that just as *reflection* influences future *preparation*, so *preparation* influences *implementation* and the whole is a continuous process.

v) Planning and organisation result in a greater degree of

involvement, participation and practice because the teacher has planned to ensure much more effective use of the time, space and equipment available. As a result higher standards of work are produced.

vi) In a carefully prepared lesson the teacher is able to cater for the varying abilities of each individual in the class and to observe the reactions of individual pupils to what is being done.

vii) Preparation is helpful in maintaining control and good discipline, because the teacher has the situation well in hand. The children know this and react accordingly; they quickly sense the teacher's certainty and security.

h   All these factors combine to produce a satisfactory and satisfying class–teacher relationship which is very difficult to achieve in lessons which are ill-prepared, disorganised, badly taught, inactive and lacking in purpose.

Much is said these days about the scientific approach to various aspects of physical education – to techniques of performance, to physiological, psychological and sociological problems, to skill acquisition and to many other facets of the work too numerous to mention here. Similarly a much more scientific approach is necessary to the problems of organisation, administration, planning and recording. These are vital factors which are often neglected to the detriment of both teachers and pupils.

5 The philosophy underlying the curriculum

The indisputable value of preparation and planning having been established, how does the teacher proceed to the planning of the physical education programme for his school? In the first instance he must be quite clear in his own mind concerning the philosophy upon which his programme is to be based. Several suggestions have already been made in respect of the principles to be followed in formulating a philosophy; for example:

Are standards of performance important?

Is variety of greater significance?

Is there a place for individual choice?

Should the programme change with the age and experience of the pupils?

Should there be preparation for post-school participation?

Is the aim to train, or to educate, or both?

What are the teaching methods to be used?

The philosophy for the school will depend upon the answers to questions such as these. All the lessons in one aspect of physical education combine to constitute the scheme of work in that particular aspect. All the schemes of work in the various aspects of physical education combine to constitute the programme or curriculum for the school. The programme of physical education, as distinct from schemes of work or lessons, provides the plan, the pattern, the outline, the formula round which the whole revolves or upon which the whole is built and developed. In their book *The Logic of Education* (Routledge and Kegan Paul, 1970), Professors P. H. Hirst and R. S. Peters state: 'we take the term curriculum to be the label for a programme or course of activities which is explicitly organised as the means whereby pupils may attain the desired objectives', whilst in *Philosophical Foundations of the Curriculum* (Rand McNally, 1967), Tom C. Venable suggests that 'the curriculum should be organised or structured in order to provide the maximum opportunity for learning'. In the Spens Report (1938) the curriculum is defined as 'in the strict sense a statement or programme of courses of teaching and instruction. A wider definition might be – all the experience which the pupil has under the guidance of the school.'

But the programme must be based on a sound philosophy which satisfies basic educational principles, and before giving guidance on the planning of a programme it is necessary to be clear about the philosophy and the principles upon which such guidance is based. During the early years of the secondary school programme it is recommended that the number of aspects to be included should be limited so that worthwhile and in some cases high standards of performance can be expected. At a later stage the programme should be widened and expanded and ultimately should lead to opportunities for some choice on the part of each pupil.

Teachers, especially young teachers, are advised to prove themselves capable of producing high standards of work in a limited field to satisfy the needs of the pupils and to convince themselves, as quickly as possible, of their own teaching ability. Confidence in themselves having been established and their ability to organise, present and develop their work satisfactorily having been proved, they will be able later to widen their programme with a greater degree of confidence and with no apparent decline of standards. The situation, which one meets so frequently, where a teacher hides under the cloak of a varied programme to the neglect of worthwhile standards, is deplored. Variety for its own sake has little value, whether in the programme as a whole, in a scheme of work, or in a single lesson.

Each teacher must plan his overall programme to make it as comprehensive as possible without sacrificing acceptable and reasonable standards. This constitutes a challenge to all teachers.

Standards of work are a reflection of the teacher's own ability and standards. High standards of work are not achieved by accident – they are the result of effective preparation; careful organisation; good teaching; consistent effort; adequate opportunities for repetition, revision, consolidation, concentration; and appropriate demands.

Similarly, poor standards are not accidental. They result from a lack of the factors enumerated above and since teachers are willing to accept recognition for producing good work and are able to enjoy the justifiable praise and the compliments which such work brings, they must also be prepared to accept responsibility for poor work and the justifiable criticism which accompanies it.

6 Stages of development in programme planning

Having decided on the philosophy, a framework upon which the programme can be built to implement the philosophy is required. The following four stages of development will provide a satisfactory framework. It must be remembered, however, that the transition from the teacher selected and controlled programme in the early stages to optional activities in the final stages is a gradual one.

Stage I
The teacher follows a limited programme with a generous allocation of time to each of the aspects selected.

In this stage the aspects to be included should be limited to enable high standards to be produced. Quality of work is the main aim – to be achieved by familiarity and repetition with a generous allowance of the available time to each of the aspects selected. Standards are reflected in depth or quality of performance rather than in the width or variety of the programme, but it is assumed that a basic course will be followed which would include gymnastics, swimming, athletics and at least one major winter and one major summer game. The programme might therefore be:

gymnastics	54	periods
swimming	13	,,
athletics	13	,,
cricket	26	,,
football	54	,,
	160	periods

It is perhaps of interest to recall that this type of programme with little if any modification was followed in most schools throughout secondary school life. Although there is much to commend such a restricted programme in the early stages it cannot be justified in the later years and it is much regretted that some schools still retain such a pattern for pupils of all ages. It is considered to be just as inadequate and educationally unsound to present such a restricted and often unpopular programme, lacking in appeal for many pupils, for the whole of the secondary school life as it is to present, at all ages, so wide and varied a programme that high standards in anything are virtually impossible to achieve.

Stage II

As in Stage I, but the teacher discriminates between classes in the choice of aspects taught.

In all teaching situations evaluation and assessment are important factors. After one year the teacher should evaluate what has been done and assess the reaction and response of the pupils to their lessons and their interest and enthusiasm for the various aspects of the physical education programme which they have experienced.

This assessment is invaluable as a guide in determining the programme for the second stage in which the teacher should discriminate between classes in selecting the different aspects of work to be included. Influenced by his assessment of the degree of success already achieved he modifies the programme for each class in order to exploit and accommodate to the full the different interests and abilities displayed. This situation could be expected to materialise in the second year of the secondary school course, when far greater emphasis will be placed on those aspects in which a class has displayed special interest or aptitude. On the other hand, less time will be allowed for those aspects which have not proved particularly successful and this might allow for the introduction of new aspects of work. As a result the teacher could find himself following a more varied programme, while at the same time each class enjoys the opportunity of a generous time allocation to those activities in which the pupils are particularly interested or to which they are being introduced for the first time. For example, Form II AB might show a particular flair for gymnastics and cricket which might not be so successful in II CD, whereas II CD might take more to swimming and could be introduced to basketball and tennis.

A suitable programme for the two forms might be the following:

	II AB	II CD
gymnastics	54 periods	27 periods
rugby football	28 periods	28 periods
association football	26 periods	26 periods
athletics	13 periods	13 periods
swimming	13 periods	27 periods
cricket	26 periods	NIL
tennis	NIL	26 periods
basketball	NIL	13 periods
	160 periods	160 periods

This is the first stage of the teacher's efforts to broaden the programme and to introduce a greater degree of flexibility and freedom in order to accommodate the varying interests of the pupils. The programme now begins to develop more widely without any accompanying lack of standards and in addition there is an attempt to accommodate individuals though still within a class structure. The interests of individuals will be further catered for by opportunities for membership of out-of-school clubs, many of which will be conducted by members of staff who are not physical education specialists. For example the keen tennis and basketball players of II AB or the talented cricketers and gymnasts of II CD would be encouraged to join these particular clubs where practice and coaching would be available.

In many ways this stage may be considered as a kind of compromise or half-way stage between on the one hand a totally teacher-dominated programme without consideration of class needs and interests, and on the other as a scheme of individual options allowing for the maximum amount of individual choice.

Stage III
The teacher follows a wide programme with a more limited allocation of time to each of the aspects selected.

The aim of Stage III is to provide a wide programme for the class in order to allow the children to experience a greater variety of activities. It is on this foundation of actual experience rather than on casual mood or fancy that the individual will ultimately be able to make his choice in Stage IV – the options stage. It is reasonable to assume that, because the teacher is now operating on a wide front, a generous allocation of time cannot be given to each of the aspects undertaken and that high standards in everything cannot be expected. Inevitably, even in these circumstances, some individuals will excel because of their natural ability and one would expect comparatively high standards in those activities in which there has been a reasonable amount of practice and coaching in previous years.

As in Stage II, greater variety can also be achieved in this stage by presenting individuals with the opportunity to join school clubs in such activities as judo, fencing, archery, badminton, table-tennis and so on. In addition, the principle of varying the programme for different classes will also apply, not only by varying the actual activities but by changing the emphasis or time allocation for particular activities.

Some teachers have found that this stage can be most successfully implemented by using the *block* method of instruction. In this method, once the time allocation for each activity has been settled, one activity only is dealt with in successive lessons – and when the allocation of time for that aspect has been completed the concentration of effort is directed to the next, until the whole programme has been covered (see Fig. 35). Seasonal factors as well as the availability of facilities (e.g. gymnasium or swimming bath) would have to be considered when planning the order in which the aspects would be taken.

On the other hand, many teachers have enjoyed success by adopting the *spread* method (see Fig. 34) whereby the concentration on any one aspect is extended over a longer period (e.g. one lesson per week continuously for several weeks rather than several lessons each week for a shorter period). No particularly strong views are held on the comparative values of these two methods of implementation because both can be very successful. The choice of method should be left to the discretion of each individual teacher. Many teachers, however, find a combination of both ideas to be most successful.

During this stage of the programme the teacher could include some or all of the following activities, all of which are suitable for presentation on a class basis:

association football	circuit training
rugby football	gymnastics
athletics	swimming
cross-country running	tennis
basketball	volleyball
cricket	

minor games (stoolball, padder tennis, skittleball, etc.)

In addition, there will be opportunities for pupils to join school clubs.

Stage IV
Optional activities for older pupils.

In Stage IV the teacher endeavours to provide opportunities for older pupils to participate in those activities in which they display particular interest and perhaps particular ability. Without any doubt this is an important stage which should be a feature of every school's programme. This is the culminating point of the physical education programme and it provides a sound preparation for post-school participation in some form of physical recreation. The implementation of this stage, because of its significance and the problems involved, will be dealt with more fully in Part Three, 'Optional Activities for Older Pupils'.

Figure 27 (page 111) illustrates for easy reference the recommended stages of development already discussed for the implementation of a school's physical education programme.

7   The influencing factors

It would be impossible and indeed undesirable to legislate for every teacher in the planning of his programme, nor would it be possible here to solve the many varied problems each has to face. The problems are individual ones relating to him and to his school, and they are affected by many variable factors. There are, however, certain basic influencing factors which must be considered by all teachers when the philosophy for the school has been established. Evaluation and assessment of these factors is essential in the planning of a successful programme, scheme or lesson.

What are these factors?   Basically, they are two-fold:
a   material and tangible; and
b   human and personal – related to both teacher and child.

a   The material, tangible factors

FACILITIES
The first important factor to be taken into consideration must be the facilities which are available and all teachers will be greatly concerned to ensure, not only that facilities of various kinds exist, but that they are maintained in a satisfactory condition and are used to the fullest possible extent. In addition, teachers must always be concerned with the possible improvement and expansion of facilities.

110

Stage I	The teacher follows a limited programme with a generous allocation of time to each of the aspects selected.

Quality is the main aim in this stage with high standards reflecting the emphasis given to each of the aspects undertaken.

Stage II	As in Stage I but the teacher discriminates between classes in the choice of aspects taught.

Quality and standards in depth are expected of each class in each of the aspects undertaken, while the teacher, in addition, enjoys greater variety in his own programme.

Stage III	The teacher follows a wide programme with a more limited allocation of time to each of the aspects selected.

Variety of experience is the aim in this stage with standards reflected in the width of the programme.

Stage IV	Optional activities for older pupils.

Relative to available facilities and staff each individual pupil, in this stage, chooses the activity(ies) he wishes to pursue. The aim is a varied programme with standards reflected in individual choice and attainment.

FIGURE 27 *A summary of the stages recommended for the development of a P.E. programme*

Only in this way will it be possible for them to aspire to the implementation of a programme which can adequately fulfil its aims and objectives. The activities to be included in the programme will, of necessity, be limited to those for which satisfactory facilities exist. No activity should be included, on a class basis, unless the facilities enable the whole class to be actively and purposefully employed, and permit maximum personal involvement and participation during the whole of the lesson. Many activities, however, for which limited facilities only are available, can be included on an individual or small group basis, when optional or club activities are being organised.

The facilities themselves can be categorised as indoor and outdoor, school and local amenity.

School facilities – indoor
Most secondary schools have a gymnasium and an assembly hall for physical education and in addition, many schools now have a sports hall, a swimming bath and sometimes squash courts. The trend towards larger schools and the provision of additional facilities in schools through the joint action of local education authorities and local councils makes this possible.

School facilities – outdoor
As in the case of indoor facilities, the provision of facilities for outdoor activities has greatly increased in recent years. Not only has the variety of provision increased but in most instances the quality or standard of the facilities has improved, giving opportunities for widening the curriculum, for developing the work to a higher standard and for accommodating the many varied interests of the pupils. The facilities available now frequently include playing fields, including grass pitches and cricket squares; hard surface playing areas; tennis courts; cricket practice wickets, including artificial surfaces; athletics tracks and athletics training areas with jumping pits and throwing areas; all-weather pitches with artificial porous surfaces, sometimes floodlit for evening use; and open-air swimming pools.

Local facilities and amenities
Teachers should make themselves familiar with suitable additional facilities which exist within the immediate neighbourhood of the school or within such reasonable distance of the school that it is possible to make satisfactory use of them. Local councils, industrial concerns and private clubs are usually most cooperative in allowing their facilities to be used by schools, but such use requires official negotiation to be conducted between the schools and the L.E.A. on the one hand and the local councils, clubs and firms on the other. Initiative should be used to exploit to the full any facilities which might be available to enable the school's curriculum to be widened.

Many schools make use of such additional facilities as playing fields; athletics tracks; sports halls and indoor cricket schools;

swimming baths – indoor and outdoor; tennis courts; squash courts; golf courses; and ice rinks. Moreover, the trend towards the provision of multi-purpose sports centres will have a great impact on future physical education programmes in schools.

Facilities for outdoor pursuits

Reference has already been made to the greatly increased interest in outdoor pursuits, but it must be realised that participation is only possible when adequate facilities in the form of natural or specially developed features are available. In most cases these features have to be found away from the school itself; they include: water (lakes, rivers, canals, reservoirs and the sea); mountains, hills and fells; rocks and rock outcrops. Many of these are now available for schools to use if they take the necessary steps to find them. Farmers and private owners, once reluctant to permit the use of their land and property for such pursuits, have in recent years shown a much greater willingness to cooperate with schools and other well-organised groups. They now realise that, in addition to the recreative and social values of these activities, the main objects of outdoor pursuits include the development of respect for the countryside and an acceptable code of behaviour.

It is possible to find facilities suitable for some or all of the more usual outdoor pursuits either at the school; in the immediate neighbourhood of the school; at a centre owned and administered by the school; at a centre owned by the local education authority; at centres owned by other authorities, organisations, or private clubs, etc.

EQUIPMENT

The amount and range of apparatus available should always be in sufficient quantities to guarantee maximum involvement and participation by each member of the group or class. The curriculum will of necessity be limited to those aspects for which the required amount of equipment is available and any expansion of the programme should only be made when the additional equipment requirements can be met. This is the second major factor to be considered when the school's curriculum is being prepared. Too frequently teachers attempt to include aspects of the programme for which there is an inadequate supply of equipment and as a result there is lack of practice, lack of progress and in time greatly diminished interest and enthusiasm. Numerous instances could be quoted to illustrate this point (e.g. a lesson in archery for a class of 30 pupils when only six bows are available, or a lesson in badminton with only eight racquets).

In such situations the activity should be organised on a small group or club basis, or during periods when optional activities for older pupils are being conducted.

SIZE OF CLASSES

Having assessed the extent of the facilities and space available and the amount of equipment at his disposal, the teacher must consider the number of pupils to be accommodated at any one time. This could vary from a small group to a class or even a number of classes. The number of pupils in a class will often determine the aspects to be included in the programme. Small classes can often be accommodated when facilities, equipment and space are limited and when safety and supervision are of special significance. Sound organisation will enable many problems to be satisfactorily solved, but it must be appreciated that in some circumstances the number of pupils involved will prohibit the inclusion of some aspects of the work. A reasoned approach to the problems of selection when large classes are involved is essential.

THE TIME AVAILABLE

As already stated, the time available for physical education in schools has not increased in proportion to the increase in the range of activities now frequently included in the curriculum. Because of the time factor alone, careful selection of aspects for the programme becomes a vital consideration, no matter how generous the provision of facilities and equipment. Selection will be influenced by the philosophy on which the programme is based and the teacher must plan so that he can use the time available to the best advantage in order to achieve the aims and objectives of that philosophy. The time factor must be considered not only in respect of the number of periods allocated to physical education in each week, term and year, but also in respect of the length of each period.

A systematic approach to the preparation of the programme is essential both in respect of the planning and recording of the work, to ensure that a satisfactory balance is kept between the various aspects included, and the time available. In this respect the use of a pro forma similar to those recommended in Figs 29 and 37 will be helpful and indeed essential if the planning is to be really systematic and successful.

TIME–TABLE PLANNING

The willingness of the headteacher to plan his time-table in order to make the best use of facilities, staff and time available is of great importance. For example, by joining several consecutive periods together to form an extended session it is possible to include such activities as sailing, canoeing, rock-climbing, orienteering, and so on, which usually require a longer allocation of time to make their inclusion worthwhile, or to justify a visit to a golf course, athletics track, or ice rink. In addition, when physical education lessons are time-tabled for the end of the afternoon session, it becomes possible to continue after school hours if desired, with obvious advantages. The successful implementation of Stage IV of the programme – optional activities, which will be discussed in Part Three – depends to a large extent on the headteacher's cooperation with regard to time-table planning.

There is ample evidence to show that more and more head-teachers consider these factors to be of great importance and prepare their time-tables accordingly.

CLIMATIC CONSIDERATIONS

Climatic considerations are an important factor when planning the programme. One would expect to find different programmes in operation in different parts of the country because of varying climatic conditions and planning must take into account the need to vary the programme according to prevailing weather conditions. The suit-ability of activities for the summer and winter seasons is an additional factor to be considered. The availability of indoor facilities during bad weather involves administrative problems, but is an important consideration when planning the programme. Planning should be sufficiently flexible to permit a change in a scheduled programme when prevailing climatic conditions warrant it.

If a programme is regarded as a guide rather than a compulsory routine it should be possible to change from an indoor to an outdoor lesson in order to take advantage of an unusual or unexpected spell of good weather and similarly to change from an outside to an indoor lesson if the weather conditions are particularly bad. This is often much more difficult if indoor facilities are limited.

LOCAL TRADITIONS AND LOCAL CLUBS

Most areas have strong local traditions in their sporting and re-creational interests and these traditions must be borne in mind during the process of planning the school's physical education curriculum. Local competitions and clubs are founded on these local interests and the range of activities followed at school should include those which will be a preparation for post-school participation and membership of local clubs. A feature of recent developments, however, has been

115

the establishment of new local clubs which have been inspired and developed as a direct result of the introduction of a wider range of activities into the physical education curriculum of the schools. Many sailing, canoeing and climbing clubs come under this category and new clubs in so-called traditional activities have been formed in areas where such activities were not traditional, e.g. rugby in a traditionally soccer area. The school's programme, therefore, whilst catering for the traditional activities of the area should not be limited only to these, but should be expanded to include additional aspects. A comprehensive programme possesses three distinct advantages from the point of view of preparing pupils for post-school recreation:

a   the development of competence in those traditional activities which flourish in the area;

b   the fostering of interest in other aspects which might lead to the formation of new clubs in the area;

c   preparation for participation in activities which, although not traditional in their own area, may be popular in areas in which the pupils might subsequently live.

The efforts of local sports advisory councils lead to greater community interest in sport and recreation and to the provision of new and improved facilities. Teachers should welcome opportunities to contribute to the work of these local sports councils and take advantage of using any facilities which might be provided as a result of their efforts and to act as liaison officers between the school and the community in matters of sport and recreation.

SCHOOL CLUBS

The existence of successful school clubs which operate during out-of-school hours will often determine whether certain aspects need to be included in the normal daytime programme. Such clubs often make it possible to implement a wider programme than could otherwise be conducted during school hours and to include activities which cater for small groups only when limited facilities make class methods of instruction virtually impossible. School clubs have several distinct values:

a   they provide opportunities for additional coaching and practice for pupils who have outstanding ability and also for pupils who, though not particularly gifted, are particularly interested;

b   they provide opportunities for the inclusion of activities for which there has been insufficient time during the normal school time-table lessons;

c   they offer opportunities for the coaching and training of representative school teams;

d   they permit the introduction of small group activities which cannot conveniently be organised on a class basis;

e   they allow additional time to be devoted to those aspects which are especially popular and for which adequate time cannot be made available during school hours;

f   many pursuits, such as sailing, rock climbing, golf, and so on, are often only possible for a club, because they have to be conducted away from school premises and the time involved in travelling usually prevents their inclusion in the normal daytime programme;

g   the club programme probably makes a greater contribution to preparation for membership of adult clubs than does the normal lesson programme because it is catering in the main for pupils with special interest, enthusiasm and ability.

The curriculum for a school must therefore be considered not only in terms of the daytime lessons, but also in terms of the very valuable additional contribution made by a well planned, comprehensive out-of-school club programme. Such programmes, however, cannot function effectively without adequate staff and generous tribute must be paid to the physical education specialists and other members of staff who give so much time and effort to organise successful school clubs. In recent years a significant development has been the expansion in the number and range of school clubs which reflect the expanding scope of the physical education curriculum.

FINANCIAL CONSIDERATIONS

Financial considerations will have a significant influence upon the planning of the curriculum because so much expense is involved in conducting a comprehensive programme. It is necessary to know what financial resources are available, but perhaps even more important to realise the considerable cost involved in the organisation and implementation of physical education today. It is certainly reasonable to assert that, compared with many academic subjects, the cost of the considerably expanded physical education programme has increased tremendously. This is generally recognised and accepted. As a result it must be acknowledged that more money is normally available but no programme can be put into operation satisfactorily without a complete understanding of the financial situation.

Expenditure

The main items of expenditure are:

a   *Equipment*

i) Because of class methods of instruction and modern teaching methods which emphasise a maximum degree of involvement and participation, a greater amount of equipment must be provided for almost all activities than was previously thought to be required.

ii) The greater variety of activities now included in the programme demands a wider range of equipment, much of which is very expensive (e.g. equipment for fencing, sailing, archery, judo, canoeing, etc.). It must also be recognised that the cost of all sports and games equipment has increased tremendously in recent years.

iii) Another expensive item to be considered is the replacement and repair of equipment. This can be a major demand on resources and, since safety factors are often involved, satisfactory upkeep and maintenance of all equipment are essential, whether it be the life jacket for water skills, the ropes for rock climbing, or the beam in the gymnasium.

b   *Travelling expenses*

Travelling expenses can often be very high and include:

i) the cost of transport to detached playing fields, swimming baths, sports centres, outdoor-pursuits centres, etc.;

ii) travelling expenses of school teams. With the increasing range of school activities there has been an expansion of the inter-school programme, making additional demands on the finances available.

c   *Hospitality*

Hospitality for visiting teams or groups must be considered. The social values of entertaining visitors are important educationally and constitute a worthwhile aspect of training, but the costs involved will need careful consideration in relation to all the other expenditures involved in implementing the programme.

d   *Affiliation fees*

Affiliation fees are normally required for membership of local, county and national school sports and games associations. The values of membership of these associations far exceed the comparatively reasonable costs involved.

e   *Insurance*

Official advice should be sought regarding the need for and the nature of any insurance cover which the school might be required to negotiate. The situation with regard to the school's responsibilities in this respect varies considerably between authorities and because of the varying nature of a school's activities it will be necessary to be quite clear about such items as third party liabilities, cover for personal injuries, and cover for damage to school or personal equipment and property.

Resources

The financial resources available will determine the extent to which any programme can be implemented. Exact information concerning the sources and amounts of money at the school's disposal is therefore necessary. What are the sources? These are usually:

(*a*) *The contribution of the local education authority* This of course varies considerably both in the amount of money available and the method of its administration. In some L.E.A.s all expenses, whether for equipment, travelling, hospitality, or other items, are met from a central fund. In others, a sum of money (usually calculated on a per capita basis) is allocated for use by the school to cover all items of expenditure for all subjects and the school itself determines the proportion of the whole which is to be made available for physical education purposes. In both these situations it is of vital importance to know not only what finances are available but also the various categories of expenditure which the amount of money available must be expected to meet. A third system involves the allocation to each school of a special allowance for physical education, calculated on a per capita basis. The actual amount of money available and the items of expenditure which have to be met from it are usually clearly indicated by the L.E.A. This system has distinct advantages, not least in importance being the fact that a guaranteed annual sum is ensured for physical education. Whatever system or method is in operation, the needs are now recognised.

The local education authority usually makes by far the largest contribution to the financial resources available, but in many instances the amount must be supplemented from other sources in order to meet the total needs of the school.

(*b*) *The school fund* Most schools have a private fund which is used for many purposes, amongst which are the additional requirements of physical education, including the provision of special items of equipment and expenses involved in the inter-school sports and games programme. The school fund is derived from a variety of sources including legacies, donations, social functions and the proceeds from school concerts, plays, film shows, fetes, galas, exhibitions and other money raising efforts, made either by the school itself, former pupils of the school, or parent-teacher associations.

119

b   The human personal factors

THE TEACHER

In any teaching situation, academic or practical, in the planning of any programme or curriculum, in the implementation of any aspect or scheme of work, or in the teaching of any lesson, there is no real substitute for able teaching. Whilst excellent facilities, modern teaching methods and potentially able children all contribute to high standards of work, the most significant, single influencing factor in education is the teacher, for 'the man is always more important than his method, his personality more important than his technique'. Personal qualities will always be of primary importance. The example set by the teacher in behaviour, appearance, effort, enthusiasm, integrity, the fact that he is generous in praise, is approachable and has an appreciative and sympathetic nature, these are some of the desirable characteristics which reflect his personality. But the factors which directly influence the planning of his programme are his philosophy; his knowledge and understanding; his teaching ability; and his interests and inclinations.

The teacher's knowledge

'A little learning is a dangerous thing' and no teacher can implement any aspect of work successfully unless he has a thorough knowledge of the subject being taught. It is wise to ensure that the programme includes those aspects of the curriculum about which the teacher has particular knowledge. Such knowledge inspires confidence and helps to establish in him a sense of security and adequacy. When coupled with conviction and belief they combine to produce a teaching situation in which the results that follow can be expected to be effective and worthwhile.

If it is thought desirable to introduce into the programme aspects about which the teacher has little knowledge it is wise for him to obtain information and guidance beforehand. Teachers should take advantage of the many courses which are now available to supplement existing knowledge and acquire more. A feature of the post-war period has been the tremendous increase in the number of courses available to teachers, conducted by local education authorities, by L.E.A.s in conjunction with the governing bodies of sport and their coaches and technical officers, by national physical education associations, and by the Central Council of Physical Recreation.

There is no excuse for the exclusion from the programme of worthwhile aspects of the work because of lack of knowledge on the part of the teacher, especially since local education authorities provide generous assistance in meeting the financial costs involved in attending courses.

The teacher's ability

Even more important than knowledge of the subject is the ability to teach it. The two elements are of course closely related, though it must be admitted that they do not always coincide. Successful teaching is related to the teacher's ability to evaluate, to plan effectively and to solve the many problems of organisation. It is also related to his powers of implementation and to his capacity to develop work from elementary to advanced standards. It is a combination also of personality, knowledge, teaching technique and the determination to demand and to expect high standards in all things, at all times.

Professor F. Musgrove and Professor P. H. Taylor in their book *Society and the Teacher's Role*[1] state: 'Pupils expect teachers to teach. They value lucid exposition, the clear statement of problems and guidance in their solution.' They go on to say of the teacher, 'whether he is providing a direct routine service for his clients, or assisting in the operation of public examinations, the teacher must be an expert technician. Philosophy is not enough. He must be skilled in the techniques of diagnosis, of evaluating the abilities and personalities of his pupils and in prescribing educational procedures in the light of this diagnosis, and for this, he must be equipped with the knowledge and experience of diagnostic techniques which enables him to provide reliable and relevant information.'

Basically, personality is a natural endowment, but by conscious effort to be more active, more inspiring and more demanding, it is possible for teachers who are not particularly gifted to improve their impact on the class. On the other hand there are other factors in good teaching which are more easily improved and developed. As already stated, knowledge can be acquired or supplemented, preparation can be more thorough and teaching techniques can be modified and perfected. Successful teaching is the art of effective coaching and it involves the skilful and intelligent use of:

a   *teacher stimulation* – verbal guidance and help;
b   *demonstration* – visual guidance and help;
c   *observation* – testing the pupil's seeing powers; and
d   *question and answer* – challenging reasoning powers and understanding.

The successful manipulation of these coaching methods as and when the occasion demands is the essence of good teaching – the hallmark of the craftsman.

[1] Routledge and Kegan Paul, 1969.

Teaching ability without knowledge can be almost as unrewarding as knowledge without teaching ability, but as teaching ability develops and knowledge is increased, standards will improve and the programme can with confidence be expanded. 'Pupils can create, improve, diversify and excel, but only if the correct atmosphere is provided. No inanimate object can create this atmosphere – a good teacher can.'

The teacher's interests and inclinations

'Enthusiasm is the fuel of success' and it is perhaps unnecessary to remind teachers that they are wise to include in their curriculum those aspects of physical education about which they themselves are particularly enthusiastic. How does such enthusiasm arise? It results from such factors as:

a   personal prowess as a performer;
b   personal pleasure and satisfaction derived from participation and personal experience even without any particular natural ability, flair or talent;
c   outstanding ability in organising, presenting and coaching;
d   the positive reaction and response of the pupils;
e   the standards produced and the successes obtained.

Enthusiasm is closely allied to a feeling of security. Conversely it is unlikely that a teacher will be enthusiastic about any aspect in which he feels insecure. Without doubt success is linked with conviction, confidence and enthusiasm. The interests and inclinations of the teacher are, therefore, important and there are many benefits to be gained when he is encouraged to follow his own bent. It should be realised, however, that there can be serious limitations to this principle.

What are these limitations? The teacher can become so engrossed in his own enthusiasm that he fails to take sufficient account of or fails to assess correctly the response of his pupils – a very important consideration. In addition, his enthusiasm could result in a programme which becomes too limited because of over-emphasis on the particular aspects in which he displays personal and special interest. His programme could, therefore, lack the blend and balance which a comprehensive curriculum would give. The impact of the teacher's own interests on the curriculum will be felt most forcibly in those earlier stages of implementation to which reference has already been made and in which it was suggested that the teacher should follow a more limited programme which allows for a generous allocation of time to each of the aspects selected, resulting in the production of worthwhile standards. In this early stage of secondary school life the pupils are at a most impressionable age and the impact of the teacher's personality, ability and enthusiasm at this time has a lasting effect. The teacher, therefore, must ensure that his own interests and inclinations produce an enthusiastic attitude which fosters enthusiasm in his pupils so that the effect will be a lasting and beneficial one. This is the foundation upon which future success is based. In the later stages of the secondary school programme, widening and expansion of the curriculum is essential, and while continuing to include many aspects in which the teacher may have particular interest it may often be necessary to add other aspects which are of particular interest to the pupils rather than to the teacher.

THE PHYSICAL EDUCATION STAFF

The trend towards larger schools brings with it two main advantages: the provision of a wider range of facilities; and an increase in the number of specialist staff available.

Reference has already been made to the ever-increasing range of facilities being provided in secondary schools. The increase in the number of specialist staff available within the physical education department produces a dual advantage.

It becomes possible not only to present a wider range of activities but also to ensure that all aspects are presented by members of staff who have particular interest and ability in these aspects. As a result the number of specialist staff available will have an extremely important influence upon the planning of the programme both with regard to the range of activities introduced and with respect to the standard of tuition. A high standard of organising and administrative ability is required to ensure the successful coordination of the programme itself and the efforts of those who implement it. This involves the cooperation and integration of all members of the physical education department and frequently programmes can be further expanded and diversified by coordinating the efforts and abilities of the men and women specialist teachers.

CONTRIBUTION OF OTHER MEMBERS OF STAFF

Further advantages can be gained, in both small and large schools, through the very useful contribution which can be made by members of staff who, though not specialists in physical education, have special interest, experience and ability in one or more aspects of physical activity. They are often very keen to make a contribution to the P.E. programme, particularly in Stage IV of the scheme when options are being considered, or in the activities of school clubs. In fact, when a comprehensive programme is being planned, it must be appreciated that success will often depend, to a large extent, upon the way in which the enthusiasm, interest and ability of all teachers are used.

AVAILABILITY OF PART-TIME SPECIALISTS

The introduction of some aspects of work into the curriculum may be dependent upon the availability of visiting part-time specialist staff and this factor will need careful consideration, particularly when planning Stages III and IV of the programme. When suitable part-time staff can be employed, the problems of expanding the programme and of allowing a greater measure of individual choice are simplified, with obvious advantages for the pupils, but it must be recognised that this can be costly. It is necessary to ensure that such part-time staff are suitable, from the point of view of qualifications, attitude and teaching methods, to operate successfully in the school situation and that they are not appointed just because they themselves are expert performers in their specialist activity. It is often felt, and not without justification in some instances, that the principle of employing staff who are not professionally trained teachers is unacceptable. Experience has shown that there are many who, though not professionally qualified, can satisfy the necessary educational requirements and who, because of their personal experience and ability, are able to make a very valuable contribution in such activities as archery, golf, fencing, rock climbing, and so on.

Though not very widely practised at the present time, it would seem logical to expect that the increasing employment of part-time specialists will be a trend of the future if elective or option programmes are to be successfully developed and expanded.

THE INTERESTS AND REACTIONS OF THE PUPILS

It is frequently asserted that the acid test of any subject, method or teacher is the response and reaction of the pupils. The interests, aptitudes and responses of the pupils themselves must therefore be considered when planning the curriculum and particularly when making essential modifications to an existing programme. It has already been stated that the teacher should consider his own interests and inclinations when preparing his programme. It is even more important for him to take into account the interests and inclinations of pupils, particularly when these are based upon actual experience, and so it is important that the teacher should ask the pupils about the success of the work being done.

'No learning ought to be learnt with bondage. Whatsoever the mind doth learn unwillingly with fear, the same it doth quickly forget.' These words are as applicable today as when they were written by the sixteenth-century educationist Roger Ascham, who for some time was concerned with the education of Edward VI, the last Tudor King.

With this thought in mind, it would be reasonable to assume that in some circumstances classes, even in the same age group, might follow a different programme as a direct result of an evaluation by the teacher of the reaction and response of the children to the work being done. Figure 27 on page 111 makes reference to the influence on the programme of the frequent and continuous assessment of the work by the teacher as it affects the developing stages of the programme.

For convenience and emphasis Fig. 28 has been included to show at a glance the many factors which influence the planning of the programme.

If it is acknowledged that all the factors discussed in this section have an influence upon the planning of the programme, it is logical to assert that great care should be taken to give them full consideration if satisfactory and successful programmes are to be devised. Teachers will appreciate that a systematic and scientific approach to planning is essential and with this thought in mind the following suggestions should serve as a useful guide to the solution of problems in the planning and preparation of the physical education programme.

8   The use of pro formae in planning

As stated at the beginning of Section 7 (page 110) it is not possible or desirable to legislate for every teacher in the planning of his programme because of the varying influence of the many factors involved. It is emphasised, however, that in order to maintain a satisfactory balance between the various aspects selected for inclusion in the programme and the time available, a systematic approach to planning is necessary and in this respect the use of an appropriate pro forma is recommended.

The year's programme for any one class

It will readily be understood that it is necessary for the teacher to give consideration not only to the actual allocation of time, but also to the number of lesson periods he intends to give to the various aspects which he proposes to include in the programme for any one class or group and the use of a pro forma similar to the one illustrated in

```
┌─────────────────────────────────┐
│     THE MATERIAL FACTORS        │
└─────────────────────────────────┘
                │
┌───────────────────────────────────────────────────┐
│  FACILITIES:                                        │
│                                                     │
│       School facilities – indoor                    │
│       School facilities – outdoor                   │
│       Local facilities and amenities                │
│       Facilities for outdoor pursuits               │
│                                                     │
│  EQUIPMENT                                          │
│  SIZE OF CLASSES                                    │
│  THE TIME AVAILABLE                                 │
│  TIME-TABLE PLANNING                                │
│  CLIMATIC CONSIDERATIONS                            │
│  LOCAL TRADITIONS AND LOCAL CLUBS                   │
│  SCHOOL CLUBS                                       │
│  FINANCIAL CONSIDERATIONS                           │
└───────────────────────────────────────────────────┘


┌─────────────────────────────────┐
│       THE HUMAN FACTORS         │
└─────────────────────────────────┘
                │
┌───────────────────────────────────────────────────┐
│  THE TEACHER:                                       │
│                                                     │
│       his knowledge                                 │
│       his ability                                   │
│       his interests                                 │
│                                                     │
│  THE NUMBER OF PHYSICAL EDUCATION STAFF             │
│  CONTRIBUTION OF OTHER MEMBERS OF STAFF             │
│  AVAILABILITY OF PART-TIME SPECIALISTS              │
│  THE INTERESTS AND REACTIONS OF THE PUPILS          │
└───────────────────────────────────────────────────┘
```

FIGURE 28   *A summary of the factors which influence programme planning*

Fig. 29 (page 128) is recommended. This type of pro forma, when completed, would indicate the number of lesson periods allocated during the school year to each aspect and it can be used either to plan a programme in advance, or to record lessons actually completed.

The information thus available enables the teacher to assess, easily and quickly, the aspects covered and the degree of emphasis placed on each and such information would influence the planning of future programmes in relation to the factors discussed in Section 7.

To illustrate the use which could be made of the pro forma, three examples are given in Figs 30, 31 and 32 (pages 129–31). The examples refer to the detailed planning of the year's work for one class, form or group during Stages I or II of the programme and show the variation which would be expected as a result of the influences of the many factors previously discussed. It must be clearly understood that these examples are purely hypothetical ones and though they are based on actual and realistic situations within our own experience they may not necessarily coincide with the requirements and circumstances of others. The important issue is to stress the indisputable values of the pro forma. The particular circumstances which exist in reference to each example given are clearly indicated on the respective illustrations. For convenience a four-period per week allocation of time for physical education in a forty-week year, which would normally follow the pattern of two single periods and one double period per week, is assumed.

It was suggested that this pro forma could be used not only to plan the year's programme in advance for any one form, but also to record the lessons actually completed. In Fig. 33 an example is given of the use of the pro forma for both these purposes. Proposed lessons are indicated by an oblique stroke across a square which represents one period, thus: ▱. Actual lessons completed are indicated by an oblique stroke in the opposite direction, thus: ◰. It will be clear from the diagram that a planned lesson which actually materialised will be shown thus: ⊠. A lesson which is included as a substitute for a planned lesson would be shown thus: ◰, while a lesson which was planned but did not materialise would appear thus: ▱.

From Fig. 33 it will be seen that twenty periods did not take place as planned though alternative activities were substituted in fourteen of these periods. When the teacher undertakes this kind of analysis he is forcibly reminded of the comparatively little time available for any one aspect of his programme and this serves to emphasise not only the need for careful planning but also for making the very fullest use possible of every period at his disposal.

PLANNING STAGE III
In Section 6 (page 106) it was suggested that in Stage III of the programme, the expansion stage, some teachers found the block method more favourable to their circumstances, that others preferred the spread method but that many achieved success by a combination of the two. Figure 34 (page 133) gives an example of the use of the pro forma in planning a programme for Stage III based on the spread

ASPECT OF P.E.	Number of periods	AUTUMN TERM week								SPRING TERM week							SUMMER TERM week						
		1 2	3 4	5 6	7 8	9 10	11 12	13 14		1 2	3 4	5 6	7 8	9 10	11 12	13	1 2	3 4	5 6	7 8	9 10	11 12	13

TOTAL NUMBER OF PERIODS–

FIGURE 29   *A pro forma for one class covering a year's work*

method and Fig. 35 (page 134) shows a programme based on the block method. It should be realised that these are examples of programmes planned in advance and that, by completing them as suggested in Fig. 33, they can also record the actual lessons taken.

In terms of time allocation, the varying emphasis given to the different aspects selected in the examples shown in Figs 30, 31 and 34 is illustrated diagrammatically in Fig. 36. This diagram also gives some indication of the comparable standards which might be expected in the various aspects covered, though these standards would obviously be further influenced by such factors as the natural ability and previous experience of the class, the quality of the teaching, the facilities, and so on.

ASPECT OF P.E.	Number of periods	AUTUMN TERM week		SPRING TERM week		SUMMER TERM week	
		1 3 5 7 9 11 13 / 2 4 6 8 10 12 14		1 3 5 7 9 11 13 / 2 4 6 8 10 12		1 3 5 7 9 11 13 / 2 4 6 8 10 12	
Gymnastics	54	////////////		////////////			
Football	54	////////////		////////////			
Athletics X.C. running	13					////////////	
Cricket	26					////////////	
Swimming	13					////////////	
Minor games							

TOTAL NUMBER OF PERIODS— 160

NOTE

(a) It will be appreciated that circumstances might necessitate minor changes in the programme, e.g. cross country running, minor games etc. might replace football or cricket when playing fields are unfit for use. These would be recorded in the appropriate section

(b) The allocation of periods to association and/or rugby football will be influenced by the policy and tradition of the school

FIGURE 30   *Pro forma: example 1 – A school with a gymnasium, a playing field, and with swimming provision limited to one period per week in the summer term*

ASPECT OF P.E.	Number of periods	AUTUMN TERM week	SPRING TERM week	SUMMER TERM week
Ass'n Football	28	///////// (weeks 1–14)		
Ru. Football	26		/////////	
Athletics	20			/////////
Gymnastics	40	/////////		
Cricket and or tennis	26			/////////
Swimming	20			/////////
X.C. running				
Minor games				

NOTE

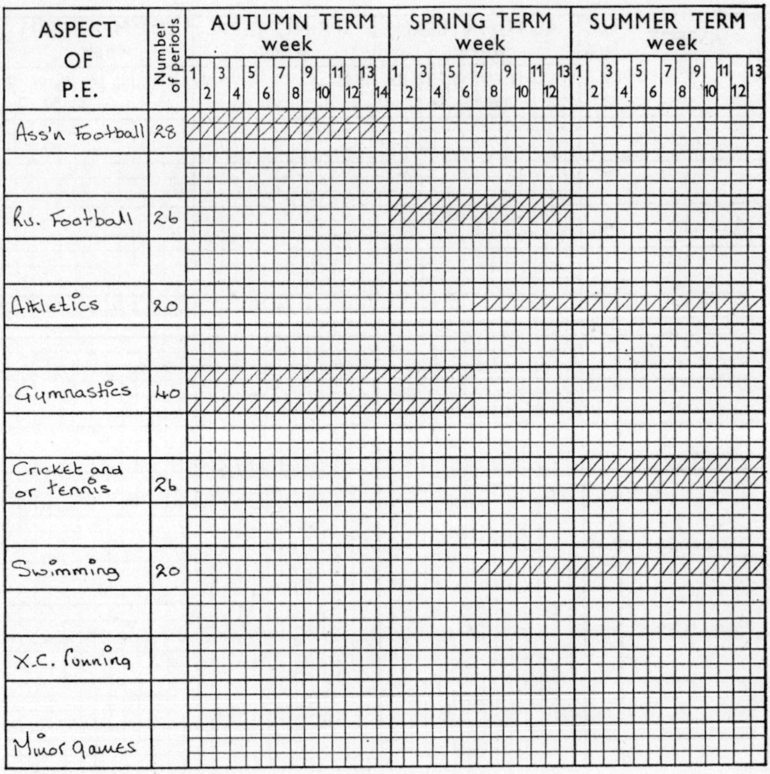

TOTAL NUMBER OF PERIODS– 160

(a) The programme will be subject to modification as suggested in Example 1 – note (a)

(b) It will be seen that in this example provision has been made for the inclusion of both association and rugby football as major winter games and for cricket and/or tennis as major games in the summer term

FIGURE 31   *Pro forma: example 2 – A school with a gymnasium, a playing field, tennis courts and with a more generous provision for swimming*

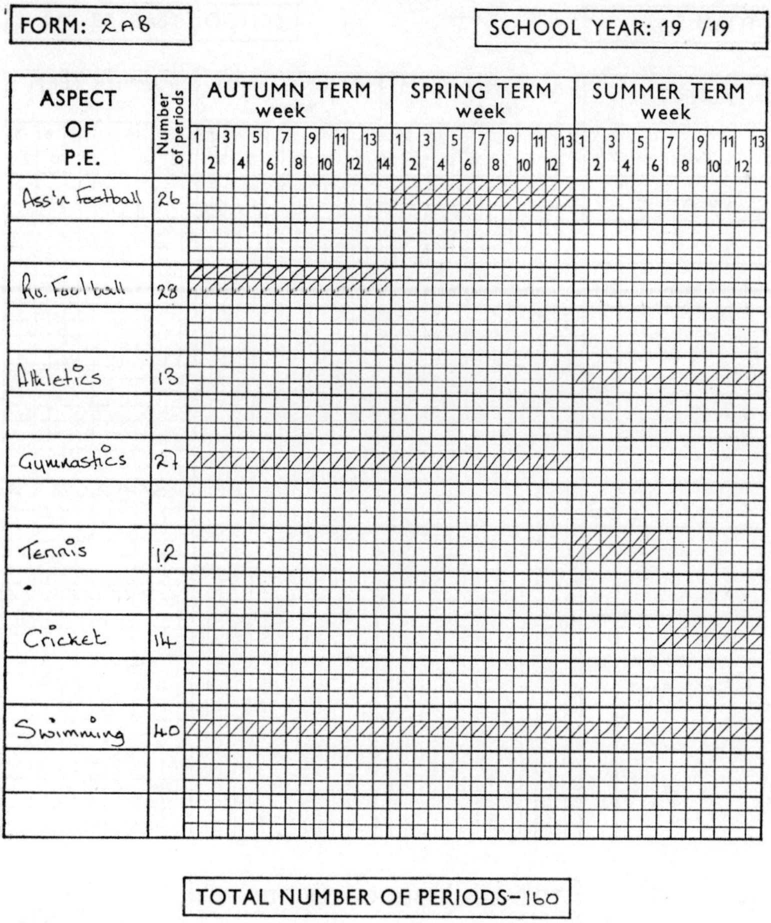

ASPECT OF P.E.	Number of periods	AUTUMN TERM week									SPRING TERM week								SUMMER TERM week							
		1	3	5	7	9	11	13			1	3	5	7	9	11	13	1	3	5	7	9	11	13
		2	4	6	8	10	12	14			2	4	6	8	10	12		2	4	6	8	10	12	
Ass'n Football	26																							
Ru. Football	28																							
Athletics	13																							
Gymnastics	27																							
Tennis	12																							
Cricket	14																							
Swimming	40																							

TOTAL NUMBER OF PERIODS—160

NOTE

Possible modifications as in examples 1 and 2—i.e. cross country running, or minor games, etc., for football, cricket or tennis when playing fields are unfit for use

FIGURE 32   *Pro forma: example 3 – A school with its own swimming bath, in addition to a gymnasium, playing fields and tennis courts*

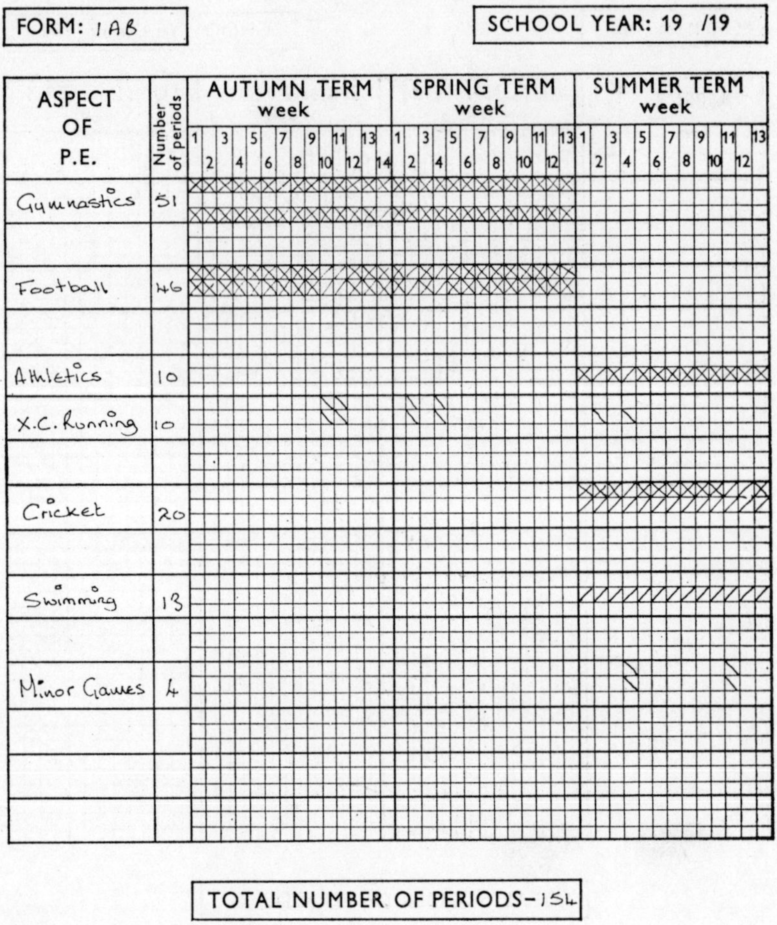
FORM: 1AB
SCHOOL YEAR: 19 /19
ASPECT OF P.E.
Number of periods
AUTUMN TERM week
SPRING TERM week
SUMMER TERM week
1 2 3 4 5 6 7 8 9 10 11 12 13 14
1 2 3 4 5 6 7 8 9 10 11 12 13
1 2 3 4 5 6 7 8 9 10 11 12 13
Gymnastics 51
Football 46
Athletics 10
X.C. Running 10
Cricket 20
Swimming 13
Minor Games 4
TOTAL NUMBER OF PERIODS–154

Key

Lessons planned and completed ☒

Lessons planned but not completed ◪

Substitute lessons ⧅

NOTE

(*a*) 6 lessons did not materialise because of half-term holidays, Christmas festivities and summer examinations

(*b*) 14 lessons were taken in substitution for those planned because of bad weather conditions

FIGURE 33 *Dual use of the pro forma for planning in advance and recording completed lessons*

ASPECT OF P.E.	Number of periods	AUTUMN TERM week							SPRING TERM week						SUMMER TERM week						
		1 2	3 4	5 6	7 8	9 10	11 12	13 14	1 2	3 4	5 6	7 8	9 10	11 12 13	1 2	3 4	5 6	7 8	9 10	11 12 13	
Ass'n Football	20																				
Ru. Football	18																				
Gymnastics	27																				
Athletics/xcl	20																				
Tennis	12																				
Cricket	14																				
Swimming	14																				
Basketball	14																				
Minor Games	7																				
Wt./Ct. training	4																				
Volley ball Padder Tennis etc	10																				

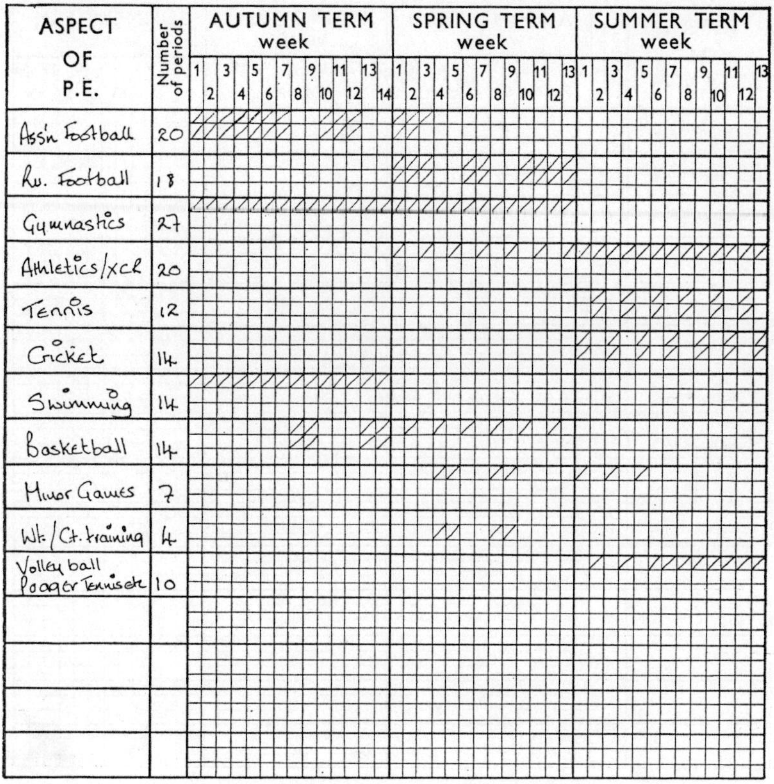

TOTAL NUMBER OF PERIODS – 160

NOTE

(a) For the double games lessons during adverse weather conditions an alternative programme should be available which might include games practices, circuit training, or additional lessons in basketball or minor games, etc., according to the facilities available

(b) Individuals will be encouraged to join school clubs which cater for those aspects in which they have particular interest

FIGURE 34 *Planning the programme Stage III – the 'Spread' method*

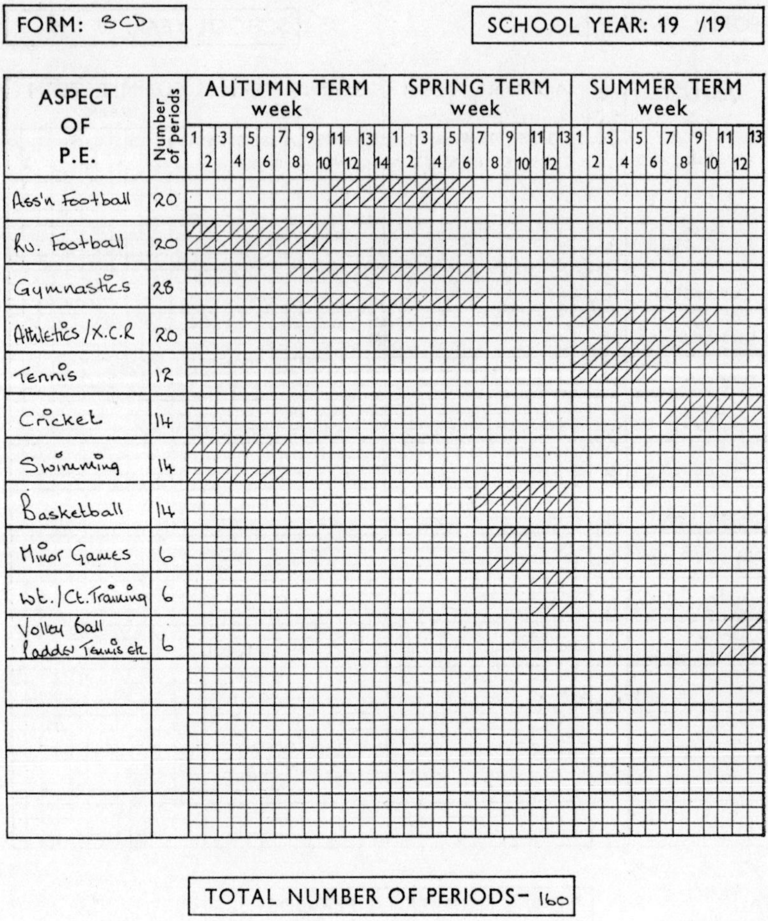

FORM: 3CD   SCHOOL YEAR: 19 /19

ASPECT OF P.E.	Number of periods	AUTUMN TERM week	SPRING TERM week	SUMMER TERM week
Ass'n Football	20			
Ru. Football	20			
Gymnastics	28			
Athletics/X.C.R	20			
Tennis	12			
Cricket	14			
Swimming	14			
Basketball	14			
Minor Games	6			
Wt./Ct. Training	6			
Volley Ball / ladder Tennis etc	6			

TOTAL NUMBER OF PERIODS— 160

See notes at bottom of Fig. 34

FIGURE 35 *Planning the programme Stage III – the 'Block' method (see notes on Figure 34, page 133)*

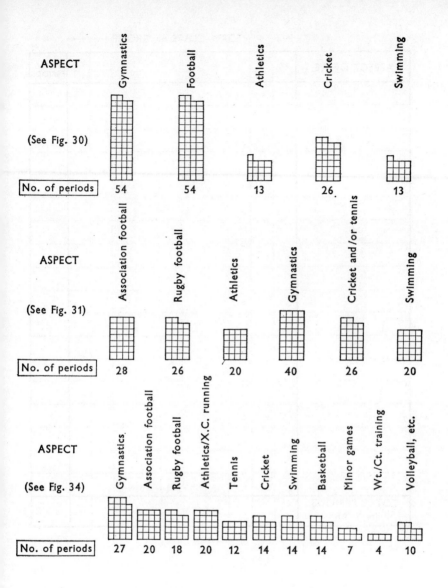

ASPECT	Gymnastics	Football	Athletics	Cricket	Swimming
(See Fig. 30)					
No. of periods	54	54	13	26	13

ASPECT	Association football	Rugby football	Athletics	Gymnastics	Cricket and/or tennis	Swimming
(See Fig. 31)						
No. of periods	28	26	20	40	26	20

ASPECT	Gymnastics	Association football	Rugby football	Athletics/X.C. running	Tennis	Cricket	Swimming	Basketball	Minor games	Wt./Ct. training	Volleyball, etc.
(See Fig. 34)											
No. of periods	27	20	18	20	12	14	14	14	7	4	10

FIGURE 36   *Allocation of time to the different aspects of the year's programme*

135

← FORM–CLASS or GROUP →

ASPECT OF P.E.											TOTAL PERIODS
TOTAL PERIODS IN YEAR											

FIGURE 37 *A pro forma for summarising the year's work of the school*

Reference to the detailed planning of Stage IV when optional activities for older pupils are arranged will be made in Part Three of this book (pages 140–80).

The year's programme for the school

Having planned the individual programme of work for each class it is valuable for easy reference to record the number of periods allocated to each aspect of the work throughout the school. This could be done by the use of the pro forma suggested in Fig. 37 which would be completed by transferring from the pro forma for each class (see Fig. 29) the details included in the column which records the number of periods allocated for each selected area of work. The advantage of this summary is that it would be possible to see at a glance a comparison of the programmes proposed for the different classes, the development of the changing curriculum throughout the school up to the completion of Stage III, and the number of lesson periods allocated to each aspect of the P.E. curriculum.

The use of this pro forma should not present any difficulties and for this reason no examples of its use are given, but it should be emphasised that an equally important use of such a pro forma would be to record the number of periods actually completed by each class in respect of each aspect of work (see Fig. 33).

The head of the physical education department of a large school will require to use an extended variation of this pro forma because of the larger number of classes concerned and the greater number of teachers involved.

9 Final comments

It has frequently been stated that the post-war period has been one of outstanding progress in the development of physical education in schools. No physical education specialist will refute this fact and in this part of the book an effort has been made to deal with one of the major problems associated with the progress made: the need for systematic planning and preparation of the expanding curriculum. Planning is an inevitable problem and because of the many factors which influence it, the solution is not easy but the moment that the teacher acknowledges the existence of the problem is the moment when progress is made towards its solution.

Emphasis has been given to the need for a well-considered and clearly defined philosophy upon which the programme is to be based and on the careful formulation of a plan or outline of the stages by which such a philosophy can be successfully implemented. The values of planning in general and the factors which influence the planning of a physical education programme in particular have been discussed in detail.

Suggestions have been given for the use of a pro forma to enable systematic planning to be carried out and examples of various types have been recommended. It must be stressed, however, that the types suggested are examples only and whilst the principle of using a pro forma is sound and should be generally acceptable, the exact design can be determined on an individual basis by either the teacher or the school. The values of the pro forma are so apparent and important that when a satisfactory type has been designed it is considered expedient for copies to be provided in quantity, and this may mean that they would have to be printed professionally and probably supplied on a local education authority basis.

The use of pro formae for systematic planning is not new, but too frequently they are not used, or are not used to the best advantage. Is it not reasonable for the teacher of physical education, no less than the specialist teacher of any other subject, to be able to indicate exactly what programme of physical education the pupils in his school are to follow, but even more important for him to be able to state accurately what programme the pupils have actually experienced and completed?

Is it not true to say that teaching becomes a much more enjoyable and satisfying pursuit when this is possible? In our experience there is only one answer – 'yes'.

Part Three

Optional activities for older pupils

1 General considerations

As frequently stated in this book, one of the outstanding developments in education in recent years, in the teaching of both academic and practical subjects, has been the use of teaching methods which successfully cater for pupils as individuals. Such methods endeavour:

a   to develop individual skill and ability to the full – a real challenge to all teachers and all methods;
b   to provide opportunities for exploration and the exercise of imagination, initiative and inventiveness;
c   to place pupils in problem-solving situations as distinct from rote-learning and mechanical instruction;
d   to motivate children through successful participation, where enjoyment and achievement become the province of all rather than the few.

The aim, it was suggested, is 'to provide a schooling structure where each child may start where he is and move as fast as his learning rate and capacity will let him'. Such developments have led to greater flexibility and freedom in teaching methods and to an improved class–teacher relationship which has resulted from the establishment of a successful compromise between regimentation and freedom, between formality and informality, and between teacher-imposed and child-centred work.

Amongst the many interesting and important features of modern teaching methods, one of the most significant is the opportunity which pupils are given to express a preference and to exercise a personal choice. One of the aims of education is to equip the individual with the capacity to discriminate and to choose wisely for himself. In a material sense democracy allows the individual the opportunity to choose from the variety of alternatives which are available. In the professional field, for example, he chooses his trade or his profession from those which are available and for which he is suited or qualified. In the domestic field he chooses his home, his furniture, his car, his music, or his entertainment from those which are available, but his choice will be further influenced by his own personal, artistic and aesthetic standards and by the material factors of cost and suitability. It must be realised, therefore, that choice is always restricted within certain limitations, that there is virtually no situation in which choice can be completely free and unlimited and that many factors, both personal and material, must be given careful consideration before an effective choice can be made.

The educational values derived from the many opportunities provided for the exercise of choice cannot be disputed. In the academic field, for example, many parallels can be drawn. A characteristic feature of modern and progressive education is the opportunity provided at nursery, infant and junior school levels, as well as at the secondary stage, for the exercise of personal choice and the expression of individuality. This is shown in numerous ways such as the freedom which children are given to choose from a variety of toys with which to play or of materials with which to work, while at a later stage and especially at sixth form level each individual makes a choice from those academic subjects in which he has had previous experience, guidance and tuition. Such choice is conditioned by the range of subjects available, by the individual's own ability and interests and by the measure of success already achieved.

This is equally relevant to physical education where modern methods permit opportunities for some degree of choice in every aspect of the programme and at every stage from the nursery school to the sixth form. Such opportunities are provided, for example, in swimming, where choice can be made from a variety of strokes or swimming aids; in athletics, where choice becomes available from a variety of events; in games, where there is frequently not only a choice of equipment or game but the need to make individual decisions in the light of changing situations; in dance, where there is the opportunity for individual response to varied stimuli, and especially in gymnastics, where, at all ages and at all stages, there are opportunities for individual interpretations of movements and activities, for individual responses to tasks and situations and for individual choice in the use made of different types of equipment.

It is equally appropriate that at the right time opportunities should be provided for pupils to choose the activities in which they wish to participate within the broader framework of the physical education programme. This enables the teacher to accommodate the varying interests and abilities of each individual pupil; and also enables each individual to prepare for the post-school period when he will be free to select activities in which to participate during periods of recreation and leisure.

This opportunity for choice of activity is now being allowed as part of the final stage in the implementation of the suggested programme of physical education as outlined in Part Two of this book. Stage IV, which provides optional activities for older pupils, is proving to be an interesting and challenging development within the physical education curriculum. In this stage, each individual is presented with the opportunity to choose from a number of available alternatives. In the realm of physical education this is a comparatively new idea, but it is fraught with many problems. In the implementation of new ideas, satisfactory answers to problems are not always easily found and in the early stages, for one reason or another, mistakes will frequently be made and failures will often outnumber successes, but it should be remembered that experimentation is frequently accompanied by temporary failure and early results may sometimes be disappointing. Much experimentation is therefore necessary, but in the hope of helping and encouraging teachers to persevere with their experimentation and to enjoy eventual success, some of the more difficult problems will be discussed and an endeavour made to solve them.

Before embarking on a programme of options the wise teacher will attempt to find satisfactory answers to the following questions:
What is meant by options?
Why optional activities in a physical education programme?
When should options be introduced?
What conditions must be satisfied?
How can options be successfully implemented?
Where should a line be drawn?

2   What is meant by options?

The word option implies the freedom to select and can be defined as:
a   the liberty to choose;
b   the power to make a selection;
c   the privilege of expressing choice;
d   the opportunity of exercising preference.
In the normal school situation and in the physical education environment of the school, all this must be in relation to that which is available as distinct from any suggestion that choice can be made without any limitation whatsoever. Options, therefore, in the context

142

of a physical education programme, refer to that stage in the programme in which the individual is allowed the privilege of choosing from those activities which can not only be made available but which also satisfy certain terms and conditions. Reference to these problems will be made later.

3 Why optional activities in a physical education programme?

The educational values of the privilege and opportunity to exercise choice have already been discussed and it has been emphasised that such opportunities are given in many ways throughout the physical education programme as a whole. Further emphasis has been laid on the fact that the freedom to choose must be carefully controlled and skilfully guided to accommodate individual variations and differences, not only in physique, physical ability and mental capacity, but also in attitudes, likes and dislikes. This has necessitated and resulted in a widening of the programme to include in the curriculum a greater variety of widely differing activities. The opportunity for individual choice and preference is extended in this final stage of the programme to a situation where each pupil is presented with the opportunity to select from the variety of physical activities which are available and which satisfy conditions which make their inclusion worthwhile. It must be emphasised, however, that there is a great deal of difference between completely free choice, a mistake frequently made by some teachers, and choice which is limited by common sense and sound reason. Extremes in either direction can be equally unrewarding. A totally teacher-dominated and selected programme on the one hand, so often a feature of the traditional physical education curriculum, and total free choice on the other, where the basic requirements of safety, supervision, active participation and adequate instruction and coaching cannot be satisfied, both lead to much dissatisfaction and frustration on the part of pupils and teachers.

In the traditional interpretation of a physical education programme, the choice of aspect at all ages was always determined by the teacher and in many cases the aspects consisted of only gymnastics and a major game in the autumn and spring terms, and a major game with either swimming or athletics in the summer term. As previously indicated, the widening of the curriculum has been a characteristic development of recent years, but the actual choice of aspects taught has still been determined by the teacher. This is the suggested plan or pattern referred to as Stage III of the programme and discussed in Part Two of this book (see Fig. 27 on page 111). Unless an options programme follows it, Stage III inevitably constitutes the final stage of the school's programme. Since greater variety is the main aim in the presentation of this stage, it constitutes a considerable improvement on the old system of one winter and one summer game, but because the choice is still determined by the teacher, even on a wide front of physical activities, only temporary satisfaction is achieved. This temporary satisfaction is experienced while the pupils are engaged on an activity for which they have ability, interest and enthusiasm, but older pupils can be resentful and frustrated when compelled to participate in activities for which they have neither aptitude nor enthusiasm. Even if the pupil's ability is limited, voluntary participation is more satisfying than compulsory participation.

Enquiries amongst older pupils have revealed that the impact of a teacher-dominated curriculum has left much to be desired. For many reasons, many pupils have lost interest in the traditional activities in which they have had to participate for a number of years, and an even more disturbing fact is that, as a result, they have lost all interest in participation in any form of physical activity or recreation when they have left school. Even the most conscientious and able teacher must acknowledge that such a result is a sad reflection on his programme and constitutes a failure to achieve one of his main objectives. On the other hand there are some pupils for whom the choice made by the teacher has been appropriate. These pupils have enjoyed and derived much benefit from their school and inter-school programme of physical activity and carried their interest enthusiastically into post-school participation. It is with the hope that such success might be shared by all older pupils that the principle of option and individual choice has emerged to constitute the final stage in the programme, a stage confidently recommended.

Enquiry of the pupils by the teacher with regard to the success or otherwise of his programme and the teaching methods used is a fundamental principle for teachers to adopt. Good teachers have always done this and have been prepared to modify both programme and teaching methods to the mutual benefit of their pupils and themselves. Questionnaires to pupils on the various aspects of the work done have resulted in information which shows surprising differences between their actual likes and dislikes and the pre-conceived ideas of the teacher. Questionnaires about what they would like to do, although a useful guide, are not always completely reliable since the answers may be influenced by factors outside the school environment (television, and so on). If, however, the selection of optional activities

144

is based on a wide experience of many aspects of physical education, then there is a greater possibility that sensible selection will ultimately be made. Stage III of the recommended programme therefore fulfils two important functions:

a it allows the programme to be expanded;

b it enables the pupil to enjoy a variety of experiences which provides him with a realisation of his interests, abilities and potentialities and the capacity, skill and discretion to make a sensible and appropriate selection from the variety of alternatives available in the final stage when optional activities are offered.

An additional advantage of a well-organised and well-planned options programme is the opportunity provided for the inclusion, in addition to the traditional aspects of the physical education curriculum, of other activities for which time and staff may not previously have been available. Reference to such activities as sailing, fencing, judo, golf, and so on will be made later; their inclusion gives the pupils greater opportunity to find some aspect of physical activity they can really enjoy and in which they can attain a worthwhile and satisfying standard of proficiency, where success may not come their way in the more traditional team sports. By the time a pupil has reached this final stage of his school life it may have become abundantly clear that he is not likely to find satisfaction from further participation in the major team games. The footballers, the cricketers, the hockey players and others, especially those who are members of school teams, usually continue to select these traditional games during their options programme. Others prefer small-side games such as badminton and tennis, non-contact games such as netball and basketball, or more individual activities such as athletics, archery, fencing and golf. Some will find greater pleasure and satisfaction from less competitive pursuits such as sailing, canoeing, rock-climbing, ice-skating, dance, and so on, and it is vital that as far as possible all these varying interests are catered for during the options programme.

Even for those who excel in major team games there are obvious advantages in ensuring that they develop an interest and some proficiency in other aspects which are more individual and less competitive. This not only leads to a broadening of interests but also provides a preparation for the time when, for one reason or another, active participation in major team games is no longer possible.

But perhaps the most important reason for the option stage of the programme is that it is a positive and direct link with possible or probable post-school participation in some form of physical recreation. It is hoped, as a result of such a programme, that by the time they

145

leave school the pupils will have decided on their likes and dislikes and will have developed an interest and achieved a measure of proficiency in those aspects which have made a special appeal. In addition, it is hoped that they will have developed the ability to choose sensibly from available alternatives so that when they leave school they will be able to become active members of local clubs or associations which offer activities in which they have had actual experience and in which they have enjoyed a degree of success. In the past too many pupils have been discouraged from joining local clubs because they are conscious of their lack of experience or ability. There is little doubt that a satisfactory options programme should enable the majority, if not all of the pupils, to overcome this problem. Certainly, it has proved to be much more successful as the final stage in the physical education programme than the more conventional procedures of the past.

4 When should options be introduced?

As already stated, there are frequent opportunities for exercising individual choice throughout school life within all aspects of the education and physical education programmes. It is necessary to decide the appropriate time when pupils should be allowed to make a personal choice from the range of physical activities available within the programme. The four stages which are recommended for the implementation and development of a physical education programme have been outlined in Part Two and are illustrated diagrammatically in Fig. 27 (page 111). It will be seen that a gradual transition is recommended from a teacher-selected and controlled programme on a comparatively narrow front, as suggested in Stages I and II, to a deliberate widening of the programme in Stage III. This pattern allows, initially, for concentration of effort on a limited number of aspects with, it would be expected, accompanying high standards, and later leads to a situation in which pupils are given a wider experience and thereby greater opportunities to realise their potential abilities and interests in some, if not all, of the aspects included in Stage III of the programme. If Stage III has been successfully implemented, the pupils will not only have enjoyed and experienced a certain amount of variety, but will be better equipped to make a sensible choice of activities in Stage IV of the programme and in the post-school years.

It is not possible to be categoric about the actual time or age when Stage III should be replaced by Stage IV – optional activities. In some schools a comprehensive and ambitious programme of options may never become possible because of adverse circumstances such as limited facilities or lack of expert coaching, but the implementation of a limited options programme would be preferable to no choice at all. Few schools will be able to complete Stage III satisfactorily soon enough to permit a change to Stage IV before the fourth year of the secondary school. It would be expected therefore that a programme which allows personal choice from a number of available alternatives might be organised during the fourth or later years of the secondary school. Whether this is possible or not will depend upon several important factors and considerations which will be discussed in the next section.

Whilst the four stages outlined constitute an ideal philosophy or plan to follow, it must be acknowledged that in some circumstances the programme, for one reason or another, cannot follow this pattern exactly. For example, Stage III might not be possible, owing to limited facilities, in which case Stages I and II could be followed by an option stage in which some choice of activity can be offered. In other circumstances one could envisage a teacher converting from a limited programme in Stage I, lasting two or three years, to an option stage identical with Stage IV. So while Stages I, II, III and IV represent ideal programme planning and progress, development as indicated below would be preferable to a programme which does not include an option stage for older pupils at the top of school:

e.g. Stage I followed by Stage II – leading to Stage IV

Stage I followed by Stage III – leading to Stage IV

Stage I – leading to Stage IV

Perhaps the most important point to remember is that any form of options programme should follow a basic course. This basic course should continue for two or three years and if possible should become broad and varied in its later stages, so that when a selection is made from the available range of activities offered, such selection is based on actual experience and knowledge. This would reflect:

a what the pupil has done;
b what he has done well;
c what he enjoys doing;
d what he hopes to do later.

To sum up then: the answer to the question 'when should options be introduced?' is threefold:

i) when the pupils have had a wide and varied experience of different aspects of physical activity to enable them to make a reasonable and sensible selection;

ii) when the pupils are old enough and are considered to be capable of making a wise and responsible choice;
iii) when the factors and conditions which govern successful implementation of an options programme can be satisfied.

5 What conditions must be satisfied?

Whilst it is agreed that the philosophy underlying an options programme is sound, and that the possibilities are almost unlimited, it must be acknowledged that the problems to be faced are considerable. The first principle to be established is that this stage of the programme is not one of soft options, but one of purposeful participation within sensible and reasonable limits. It is recommended, therefore, that an optional activities programme should never be introduced until certain conditions can be satisfied. What are these conditions? What are the prerequisites which are essential to the successful implementation of an options programme? There are three basic prerequisites:

a   adequate facilities and equipment;
b   adequate coaching and staffing;
c   thorough organisation and efficient administration.

In Part Two, the factors which influence the planning and presentation of the physical education programme as a whole were discussed in considerable detail. These included:

a   facilities;
b   equipment;
c   size of classes;
d   time available;
e   time-table planning;
f   climatic considerations;
g   local traditions and local clubs;
h   school clubs;
i   financial considerations;
j   the teacher;
k   the physical education staff;
l   contribution of other members of staff;
m   availability of part-time specialists;
n   interests and reactions of pupils.

Though these factors influence the planning of the programme at all stages, some of them have particular significance and require to be given special consideration in relation to the implementation of a successful options programme.

148

Facilities

Since this is the final stage of the school programme, since in most instances there has been previous opportunity for practice and coaching in a variety of physical activities, and since participation results from personal preference and choice, it is expected that standards of performance will be comparatively high. The facilities available therefore should be of a quality which will permit the maintenance and further development of such standards. Sub-standard facilities are not conducive to sustained interest and enthusiasm and detract from the possibility of pupils improving their performance. For example, cricket pitches, tennis and badminton courts should be good playing areas on which one could expect worth-while standards to be reached. Unless the facilities for any particular activity are of a reasonably high standard it is considered wise to omit that activity from the range to be offered. In addition to the quality of the playing areas available, it is essential that these areas should be sufficient in number to permit those taking part to enjoy maximum opportunity for practice. For example, the number of badminton or tennis courts available should be sufficient to enable all members of the group to be active without the need to wait for turns. Whilst improved class methods of instruction in many aspects of physical activity have made it possible to accommodate a larger number of pupils in a limited space, when tactical practices and competitive play are embarked upon, it is important that the best possible range of facilities should be available.

Inadequate facilities within the school need not, of necessity, limit the scope or range of activities to be offered. Suitable facilities may often be found within the immediate vicinity of the school – for example, swimming baths, tennis courts, an athletics track, a large sports hall, playing fields, local water areas. Some schools find it possible to combine with one another in the planning of their options programmes so that all the facilities of the schools involved become available for use. One example of such planning and cooperation in the joint use of facilities illustrates this point. Three schools combined and organised:

a   trampolining and gymnastics at school 'A';
b   fencing and golf at school 'B';
c   archery at school 'C';
d   swimming at the public swimming baths;
e   athletics at the college of further education stadium.

This type of organisation presents tremendous opportunities and exciting possibilities for expanding the programme and so making the fullest use of the facilities which exist within a particular area. The provision of local authority multi-sports centres which provide excellent facilities for a wide variety of activities has been a recent trend, and such centres are ideal for the implementation and expansion of the programme as a whole and a scheme of options in particular. In Part One reference was made to the variety of facilities also being provided in larger secondary schools. In effect, these facilities constitute the equivalent of a sports centre and make it possible to organise a comprehensive options programme within the school itself. Many large schools throughout the country now possess a wide range of facilities which enables them to organise a satisfactory elective programme – gymnasium; school hall; sports hall; swimming bath; playing fields; tennis courts; hard playground; athletics track and training area; cricket squares and practice wickets; and all weather pitches. How pleasing it is to imagine the possibilities offered in a school which possesses such a wide range of facilities, but even without such generous provision, many schools have succeeded in organising this final stage of their programme satisfactorily by:

a   combining their own facilities with those of their immediate neighbourhood;
b   cooperating with neighbouring schools in the use of their joint facilities;
c   combining the facilities of neighbouring schools with other facilities in the locality;
d   using local authority sports centres;
e   using appropriate facilities for various aspects of outdoor pursuits.

Every endeavour should be made to make maximum use of all the facilities available within the vicinity of the school. Care should be taken, however, to ensure that the programme includes only those activities for which the facilities are sufficiently adequate and suitable for the development of worthwhile standards of performance.

Equipment

The amount and range of apparatus available must always be in sufficient quantities to guarantee maximum involvement by each member of the group. Unless this is possible, the activity should not be made available as an option. Interest and progress are difficult to maintain if equipment is in short supply. The amount of equipment available for activities such as table-tennis, badminton, fencing, golf, tennis and so on will therefore determine the size of the group and whether or not the activity should be included in the options.

Expansion of the physical education programme as suggested in Stages III and IV demands a wide range of equipment, much of which is extremely expensive. It is not difficult to realise that the financial burden is often so great that some items of equipment cannot be made available and this constitutes the second major material factor to be considered when deciding on the content of the programme at this stage. On the other hand there are several ways in which the school's normal stock of equipment can be supplemented in order that particular activities can be considered for inclusion in Stage IV; for example:

a   cooperation between schools so that equipment at one school might be used by pupils of neighbouring schools;

b   provision of extra or special equipment from private school funds or from the fund-raising efforts of parent–teacher associations, etc.;

c   provision of personal items of equipment by individual pupils.

Every possible avenue of approach should be explored to discover ways in which the normal stocks of equipment can be increased and expanded in order to make available activities which might otherwise have to be omitted.

Coaching

Successful implementation of an options programme demands a high level of effective coaching. Unsupervised 'play' has no place in an options programme during normal school hours though it may well find a place during out-of-school activities. Those in charge of a group should be competent coaches of the activity for which they are responsible and as a result one would expect to find a progressive scheme of work in operation which provides maximum opportunity for practice, together with a satisfactory standard of efficient instruction and coaching. Too frequently, older pupils are left unsupervised to play, and though this may well be of recreative benefit and the individual has had the advantage and privilege of expressing a personal preference, in the context of a school's options programme it has limited value, because it ceases to be an effective learning situation. Moreover, it is an inaccurate interpretation of what is intended and required – options should never become 'soft' options.

Staffing

The need for adequate coaching presents a staffing problem, because in order to include and gain the fullest benefit from any particular aspect a competent coach must be provided. Even when adequate facilities and equipment are available, an activity might have to be excluded because competent instruction and coaching are not available.

The problem can be solved in a number of ways, but it must be accepted as a basic principle that a successful physical education options programme for older pupils demands a higher staff–pupil ratio in much the same way as that which exists in the academic field. This is necessary, particularly in such activities as fencing and rock-climbing, because of the need for special safety precautions, because of the need for careful supervision, and because of the necessity to provide expert tuition on a more individual and personal basis.

SPECIALIST PHYSICAL EDUCATION STAFF

The first step is to ensure that the interests and abilities of the specialist physical education staff are used to the best advantage. This involves careful consideration not only of their instructional and coaching abilities but also of those qualities which influence the successful organisation and effective administration of the programme. It involves the cooperation and integration of all members of the physical education department and frequently the options stage of the programme can be materially expanded and diversified by careful coordination of the efforts and abilities of both men and women specialist teachers.

SUPPLEMENTARY PHYSICAL EDUCATION STAFF

Many members of staff who are not trained physical education specialists often have special interest and ability in particular aspects of physical activity and because of this they are frequently very keen to make a positive contribution to the physical education programme, particularly in Stage IV. It is vital to the success of a comprehensive options programme that the valuable contribution which such teachers can make should be used to the full to supplement the work of the specialist staff.

PART-TIME SPECIALIST STAFF

Because of the high staff–pupil ratio which is so essential in Stage IV of the programme it is often found that the specialist physical education staff, even when supplemented by other members of the staff, are not sufficient in number to make the implementation of a fully comprehensive scheme of optional activities possible. It is sometimes found that even where facilities and equipment are available and there is a great deal of interest shown by the pupils in a particular activity, no member of the school staff is available to give the instruction and coaching required. In such situations the problem can sometimes be solved satisfactorily by the employment of visiting specialist staff in a part-time capacity. It must be realised that this solution to the problem may not be possible on financial grounds because money is not available to pay the professional fees involved, but even if there are no financial difficulties this problem must be given careful consideration from another point of view. It is strongly felt in many quarters that all teaching, irrespective of the subject, should be in the hands of trained and qualified teachers and that part-time specialists should therefore also be trained and qualified teachers. Though this view is worthy of support, such teachers are not always available and in fact they are usually very difficult to find. Moreover, there are often specialists available who are not trained teachers but whose personal qualities and technical ability, as well as their experience, enable them to make a valuable contribution. The availability of courses conducted by national coaches and the existence of the national coaching schemes of the governing bodies of sport have enabled many expert performers to become very expert coaches and it is appropriate that the fullest use of their services should be made, especially in this final and more adult stage of the school's programme. The employment of the part-time specialist who fits into the school situation satisfactorily can be fully justified because of the opportunity provided for the inclusion in the programme of activities which otherwise would have to be omitted. Generally speaking, the part-time specialists would be employed to deal specifically with those activities which do not usually find a place in the normal school programme, e.g. golf, archery, fencing, and so on. In other words, their services permit the introduction of aspects which are 'additional to the traditional'. The employment of part-time specialist staff can, however, be justified for at least two other reasons, even if they are made responsible for traditional activities – to increase the staff–pupil ratio, and to enable members of the school staff to take the responsibility for any non-traditional activity in which they might have special ability.

It will be seen that three categories of staff can make their own particular contribution to an options programme, i.e. specialist physical education staff; supplementary physical education staff; and part-time specialist staff. The overall success achieved will to a large extent depend not only upon the number of staff available at any one time but also upon the effectiveness with which their individual contributions are coordinated. The summary on page 154 should serve to illustrate these points and to indicate progressively the different

The specialist physical education staff of the school
(men and women operating separately)

The specialist physical education staff of the school
(men and women combined)

Physical education specialists plus supplementary staff
(men and women operating separately)

Physical education specialists plus supplementary staff
(men and women combined)

Specialist P.E. staff plus visiting part-time specialists
(men and women operating separately)

Specialist P.E. staff plus visiting part-time specialists
(men and women combined)

P.E. specialists plus supplementary staff plus part-time
specialists (all working in combination)

Combining the available P.E. staff of neighbouring schools

ways in which the services of the various members of staff can be
used separately and in combination with one another.

In many schools valuable use is made of older and responsible
pupils to supervise some of the activities taking place. This help
usually takes the form of supervising small groups during particular
practices. On occasions these older pupils have been known to make

a worth-while additional contribution by assisting in the actual coaching, thus improving the staff–pupil ratio and sometimes making a wider range of activities possible.

These suggested solutions to the staffing problem can only become effective with the support and enthusiastic cooperation of the headteacher. Even when adequate staff, suitable facilities and sufficient financial resources are available, the headteacher must be so completely convinced of the soundness of the educational principles involved and the social, physical and recreational values derived from this kind of programme, that he is willing to undertake the task of planning and frequently modifying his time-table to enable the programme to be implemented. This is no mean task, involving as it does an organisation which ensures that staff, facilities and equipment, as well as the pupils concerned, are all available at the same time. Experience shows that an increasing number of headteachers display an enthusiastic interest in optional activities for older pupils and willingly undertake the complicated organisation and administration which are necessary for the smooth and effective running of the scheme. A satisfactory solution to the staffing problem is unquestionably the predominant factor in the successful implementation of an options programme and is entirely dependent upon the wholehearted support of the headteacher.

The size of the group

The number of pupils in any one group is closely related to the problem of staffing. If the principle is accepted that coaching must be available for each group, it is important that the group should be large enough to justify the services of the teacher in charge. It would be impractical to provide competent coaches for a large number of very small groups practising different physical activities. On economic grounds alone it is therefore recommended that no group should be fewer than twelve in number unless exceptional circumstances prevail, such as the availability of competent voluntary instruction. In planning the options programme it is essential that careful thought is given to the appropriate size of the group, bearing in mind such factors as safety, adequate supervision, the availability of equipment, the importance of effective instruction and the need for active participation. For some activities, such as golf or fencing, a group of twelve to sixteen pupils would be reasonable and appropriate for one teacher to supervise and help. Other activities, such as association and rugby football, cricket or tennis, could just as satisfactorily be organised in larger groups which could be sub-divided into smaller groups for coaching and practice purposes. This is an important point to remember when considering the staff–pupil ratio and the range of activities to be offered, because those activities which can be operated in large groups compensate for those which it is far more beneficial and practical to conduct in small groups. Apart altogether from the questions of finance, availability of staff and so on, it is considered that no activity can justifiably be included in the programme unless at least twelve pupils express a firm desire to follow that pursuit. This final stage of the programme is organised on the basis of personal preference, but unless an activity can find support from at least twelve pupils it is not considered worthy of inclusion in the range of alternatives offered.

The time factor

Whether the selected activity has been experienced previously or is being introduced for the first time, it is essential that it should be pursued for a period of time long enough to enable the individual to make significant progress. If the activity has been experienced previously it has probably been chosen because of a desire on the part of the individual pupil to improve his personal performance still further and adequate time is required for this to be accomplished. The options programme, on occasions, makes it possible to introduce certain activities which for reasons of staffing, facilities, equipment, finance, supervision, it has not been possible to include earlier. If an activity has been chosen because it is new, sufficient time must be allowed for some competence to be developed or for a sound judgement to be formed, based on a reasonable amount of experience. For these reasons it is suggested that most activities should be continued for a full term and that only in exceptional circumstances should a shorter period be considered. For example, when an activity for which facilities are limited proves to be in great demand, it would be sensible to limit participation to half a term in order that the needs of other interested pupils can be met later. If there is ample evidence to show that there is sustained interest in an activity which is extremely popular but for which facilities are inadequate, every endeavour should be made to improve the facilities in order to satisfy the demand. Such situations emphasise the merits of continuous evaluation and assessment of pupil reaction to the different aspects of the programme, for this provides the surest guide to subsequent planning. There is certainly nothing to commend the practice sometimes followed where the teacher says, 'What would you like to do today?' For both teachers and pupils this is a most unsatisfactory way of organising an options programme because of the lack of repetition, continuity, worth-while practice and progress.

But is there not another important issue involved? Pupils should be encouraged to stand by the choice they have made for a reasonable length of time, rather than relinquish it because of apparent lack of success or interest. The privilege of having the opportunity to choose is sound but should not be abused. Quick capitulation should be discouraged because it is in direct opposition to the desirable development of personal qualities of perseverance and determination. Pupils should be trained to realise and accept the fact that when making a personal choice they are at the same time undertaking a personal responsibility. The need to discriminate with thought and care must be established and pupils must appreciate that the process of exercising their personal preferences must not be undertaken lightly. This is training for life and for living and if children can be trained to choose wisely and with care they are undergoing a most valuable educational experience which will be of great value and lasting benefit throughout their lives.

SINGLE AND DOUBLE PERIOD OPTIONS

A further consideration in respect of the time factor is related to the length of the lesson, that is, the single-period or the double-period lesson. Optional activities can be successfully organised in single-period lessons. Sometimes this is made more difficult to implement satisfactorily because of the fact that choice might have to be limited to activities which one teacher, responsible for a class unit, can organise, supervise and coach himself, without assistance from other members of staff. Many examples could be given from personal experience of successful single-period programmes. Five such lessons conducted in sports halls are outlined below and are illustrated diagrammatically in Fig. 38 on page 158.

Example 1: Five-a-side football, table-tennis and badminton
Example 2: Cricket net practice, trampolining and judo
Example 3: Basketball, golf net practice and football practices
Example 4: Volleyball, gymnastics and badminton
Example 5: Trampolining, table-tennis, badminton and football practices

A very successful single-period outdoor lesson involved volleyball, basketball and cricket net practice, but careful consideration of the basic principles of providing suitable facilities, adequate supervision and coaching is essential when deciding what activities to offer and how many of these activities can successfully operate at any one time. If one teacher is conducting an options session on his own he must

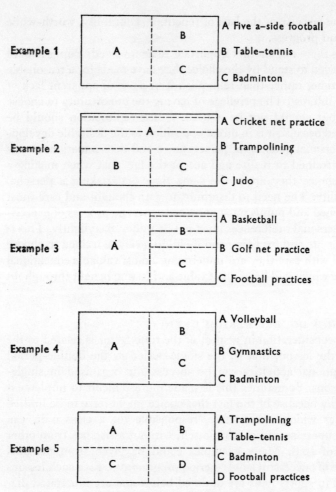

Example 1	A Five a–side football B Table–tennis C Badminton
Example 2	A Cricket net practice B Trampolining C Judo
Example 3	A Basketball B Golf net practice C Football practices
Example 4	A Volleyball B Gymnastics C Badminton
Example 5	A Trampolining B Table–tennis C Badminton D Football practices

FIGURE 38 *Single period options conducted in sports halls*

ensure at all times that he is in a position to supervise all sections of the class. This precludes any suggestion that one teacher can supervise work being conducted both inside and outside. This is most important not only from the safety point of view but also because his very presence encourages maximum concentration and effort.

The basic principles and conditions which apply to a programme of optional activities for older pupils can be better satisfied during double-period lessons when activities are organised on the basis of group participation within a multi-class or year structure rather than a single-class unit. In such circumstances most physical activities

158

would be appropriate. For example, a winter programme might include gymnastics, trampolining, association and rugby football, hockey, netball, basketball, cross-country running, fencing, and badminton, and in the summer term athletics, cricket, tennis, swimming, volleyball, golf, archery would be appropriate. In other words, seasonal considerations and climatic factors will affect the planning of the programme. If the double period is at the end of the afternoon session there is the additional advantage that the activities can be continued after school hours without interfering with the normal school time-table.

Some schools have included outdoor pursuits, such as campcraft, canoeing, sailing, rock-climbing, orienteering, in their optional programmes with considerable success. These pursuits often require more time than a double-period lesson not only to ensure satisfactory participation but also to allow any additional travelling time that may be required. Because of the obvious advantages to be gained, head-teachers have in many cases been prepared to modify their time-table to allow more time to be available for the options programme (for example, a whole afternoon).

HOW MANY ACTIVITIES FOR EACH PUPIL?
Closely related to the time factor is the question of how many activities an individual pupil should be expected or encouraged to follow in the final stage of the physical education programme during which choice is allowed and selection made. It has already been suggested that under normal circumstances an activity, once it has been chosen, should be pursued for approximately one term in order that the pupil can have time to be clearly aware of his progress and that the teacher can see some tangible results from the organisation of the programme and from the tuition and coaching which have been given. This leads to the assumption that in one year each individual would normally follow three different aspects. Certain factors which influence and modify this situation have already been discussed. For example, it might only be possible to follow any one activity for a period of shorter duration than one term, which may result in more than three activities being pursued during the year. Many schools, whose pupils remain at school beyond the statutory school leaving age, find it possible to extend the organisation of their options programme so that it covers a period of two years or even longer. They have then to decide whether a pupil must choose completely different aspects in the second or subsequent years; or whether a pupil should be allowed to enjoy for a second time an activity which he has previously selected. It is neither possible nor desirable to be categoric about this

situation because of the varying circumstances in each school. Many human and material factors influence planning and because of these factors it is unlikely that different schools would find identical programmes equally successful.

As a general rule it is felt that a pupil should enjoy at least three different activities during a one-year options programme and that in any subsequent year he should include at least one new aspect, even if repetition of previously selected activities is permitted. In other words, though the principle of repetition is supported, it is felt that an extension of the range of activities experienced by each individual is equally valuable. If the options programme is to make its full contribution to the preparation for post-school leisure time activity it must do two things:

a   provide the individual with the opportunity to develop an interest in a variety of physical activities; and

b   develop in the individual prowess and skill in his selected activities in order that he may confidently continue participation in more adult situations.

Though variety for its own sake cannot be supported, individual experience during the options periods should not be too restricted or repetitive. After leaving school it may not be possible, for several reasons, to participate in a particular activity and it is obviously helpful if experience of several activities has been enjoyed in the options stage of the programme. For example, if a dedicated enthusiast has been allowed to spend all his summer optional activity time in sailing he will be placed in an unhappy situation if for any reason he finds himself unable to participate in sailing when he leaves school. It is advisable therefore to ensure that pupils experience several activities during this stage of the programme so that later they may find themselves in the position of being able to select their leisure-time pursuits from a number of activities in which they have developed an interest and have enjoyed a measure of success.

Financial considerations

It is almost superfluous to state that the implementation of an options programme in physical education, no less than the implementation of any aspect of education or of education as a whole, is dependent upon and controlled by the financial resources available. So far as the options programme in physical education is concerned, particular financial commitments include:

a   the provision of adequate supplies of equipment;

b   payment of fees to visiting part-time specialist staff – if employed;

c   hiring of facilities not available within the school environment;
d   travelling expenses.

Since the amount of money for the options programme will of necessity be limited, very careful consideration must be given to the best use of whatever funds are available. The money spent on this part of the programme must bear a reasonable relationship to the total amount available for the overall physical education programme of the school. Since the aim should be to provide the greatest good for the greatest number, any expenditure of money at this stage should not be at the expense of the earlier stages where class methods of instruction are in operation.

PROVISION OF EQUIPMENT

The purchase of expensive items (such as a judo mat, or archery or fencing equipment) should not mean an inability to provide other items (such as hockey sticks, athletics equipment and so on) which are required for the effective implementation of the more traditional aspects of the programme. Generally speaking, modern methods of teaching have been accompanied by the provision of more generous supplies of equipment and since this equipment is available for use during the options periods, it is reasonable to assume that there would normally be no need to provide much extra equipment for such activities as football, netball, hockey, cricket, athletics, tennis, swimming, basketball, volleyball, and so on. Unfortunately, other specialist items required during the option stage to supplement the school's normal stocks are usually very expensive and it is in this respect that careful consideration must be given in order to balance the budget successfully.

At the option stage the normal stock of equipment can, if necessary, be satisfactorily supplemented by the provision of personal items by the older pupils themselves and although additional equipment will often be required to increase the range of activities available, care must be taken to ensure that a fair compromise is reached to provide for the needs of pupils of all ages and at all stages of the programme.

Another consideration to be borne in mind is the need to avoid expenditure of money on expensive items of equipment which might have only temporary or casual use. It is not uncommon to find expensive equipment for fencing, archery, or weight training (or other pursuits), purchased at the request of an individual teacher, later unused and neglected because the teacher concerned has left the school or because interest in the activity has diminished to a marked degree. Under these circumstances an exchange of equipment between schools might be possible, for transference of the items involved to a school where good use can be made of them would be preferable to no use at all. Further consideration should also be given to the possibility of excluding a particular activity from the options programme if the supply of equipment is insufficient to ensure full participation by the pupils in the group, or if the equipment available is of an unsatisfactory standard.

PAYMENT OF FEES TO PART-TIME SPECIALISTS

Reference has already been made to the valuable contribution which can be made to the success of the options programme by the employment of part-time specialist staff. Unfortunately this involves additional financial expenditure in the payment of fees for their services. Sometimes these fees can be met from the normal funds available for the payment of teachers' salaries and this means that the money available for the physical education programme is not adversely affected. Where payment cannot be arranged in this way, the fees required may be met in several ways:

a from the school's allowances for the physical education programme;

b from any private school funds which are available;

c from personal contributions by the pupils or from a combination of any of these three sources.

As in the case of the purchase of additional equipment, the money spent on additional staff should be sensibly related to the financial requirements of the programme as a whole and the employment of part-time staff should not be contemplated if this has a detrimental effect on the overall basic needs of the total physical education curriculum.

HIRING OF SPECIAL FACILITIES

It has already been suggested that the content of this stage in the school's physical education programme can frequently be enriched by the use of facilities beyond the environment of the school. These include playing fields, athletics tracks, sports halls, swimming baths, tennis and squash courts, golf courses, and ice rinks. The hiring of such facilities is usually undertaken by the local education authority and therefore the expense involved does not become the direct responsibility of the school. Occasionally, however, it may become necessary for a school to consider the hiring of certain facilities which for a number of reasons, cannot be made available by the L.E.A. In such circumstances the school may consider it worth while to meet the cost of hiring these facilities because of the obvious enthusiasm of the pupils, because the expense can be met either by the school or the pupils themselves and because such expenditure has no detrimental effect on other aspects and other stages of the programme. These are the conditions which must be satisfied, and when they are, the expense is fully justified and the activity concerned is worthy of inclusion.

TRAVELLING EXPENSES
Enthusiasm for a particular activity can sometimes lead to financial involvement which may not be justifiable in relation to the total cost of the programme. Travelling to a detached site or remote centre can be particularly expensive and before an activity which will involve transportation to any marked degree is included, very careful consideration must be given to the cost. In this part of the programme the needs of comparatively small groups of pupils are being considered when participation in any one activity is being planned and if the group can be transported at reasonable cost there could be ample justification for including such activities as golf, rock-climbing, sailing and swimming. But the needs of the majority of pupils rather than the few must be the first and most important consideration and in planning the curriculum as a whole, exceptionally high travelling expenses for any one particular options group should, if possible, be avoided, especially if the financial resources of the school are limited.

Few schools can plan their options programme without giving the financial implications very careful thought and the different aspects of expenditure involved must be clearly appreciated. A wide range of activities is recommended but there is an important condition to be satisfied. It is suggested that activities should not be included if they make such an exceptional demand on the financial resources available that their inclusion leads to a diminished standard of provision for the remaining and equally important parts of the school's physical education programme. When the financial resources available allow for expansion in the range of alternative activities the results are commendable.

Opting out of physical education

'Should older pupils be allowed to opt out completely from the physical education programme?' This is a question often posed by headteachers and others. Our answer to this question is, of course, 'No', and it is confidently assumed that this would be the answer of all physical education teachers and indeed of educationists generally. It is realised that there are some who would assert that if choice is allowed and this principle is taken to its logical conclusion, then the individual should be allowed to decide to opt out of physical activity altogether and to substitute some other aspect of the curriculum, either academic or practical. To permit this to happen would be to acknowledge a lack of value in physical education, either physical or educational, and amounts to an admission that physical education makes no valid contribution to education as a whole.

The reasons for the inclusion of physical education in the school curriculum and the advantages of all that is implied in a modern interpretation of physical education have been discussed frequently in this book and in many other publications dealing with the principles and philosophy underlying its presentation. It is unnecessary to repeat these arguments here, but merely to re-assert the conviction that physical education is an integral and essential part of education. It is contended that whilst physical education can justify a prominent place in the curriculum at all levels, it is perhaps even more important to ensure its inclusion for older pupils who are frequently subjected to academic responsibilities and to social and emotional pressures and stresses of many kinds. One important condition to be satisfied, therefore, is that all pupils, unless exempt on medical grounds, should participate regularly in some form of physical activity and that when choice is allowed the pupils should not be allowed to opt out, resulting in no participation at all.

The principle to be established in an options programme is that the pupil is allowed the privilege of choosing from a number of available alternatives. To opt out of the options programme is diametrically opposed to the principle of choice, because opting out is not one of the alternatives offered. Compulsory participation without choice, a feature of conventional or traditional programmes, is the direct opposite of a situation in which there is no participation at all. Of these two extremes, the former is to be preferred since some value must be derived from participation, even if teacher-directed, but a well-organised options programme is, for the many reasons previously given, much more desirable.

To sum up, then – if, as a result of allowing choice, a point is reached when some pupils wish to opt out, the real value of an options programme is lost and its purpose virtually defeated. Such a situation could be a reflection of the unsuccessful and unsatisfactory nature of the programme and the ineffectiveness of the organisation.

Administrative requirements

No aspect or stage of the physical education programme can succeed without effective planning and preparation, and the final stage (the options stage) is no exception. In fact, the many conditions which have to be satisfied to ensure success indicate that this stage demands even more careful and efficient administration and organisation than any other part of the programme. The reasons should be clearly apparent, because the aim is to provide for the many varying interests of individuals, rather than for the needs of a class unit. The administration required for the successful organisation and development of the options programme is both challenging and demanding, and will be fully discussed in Section 6 where it is hoped to answer in some detail the question: 'How can options be successfully implemented?'

It is sufficient here to indicate that the existence of efficient administration is an important condition which must be satisfied if a successful options programme is to be carried out. Many unsuccessful and unsatisfactory programmes are seen where:

a   the facilities are not of a sufficiently high standard;
b   equipment is in short supply, resulting in limited participation;
c   supervision is non-existent;
d   coaching is limited in both quantity and quality;
e   standards of dress are poor and are reflected in poor standards of performance;
f   there is a lack of continuity and progress.

Such programmes are a direct result of:

a   inadequate assessment of the factors which influence and determine the range of activities offered;
b   inadequate realisation of the conditions which have to be satisfied;
c   ineffective preparation, organisation and administration.

It is not surprising under these circumstances to find much adverse criticism of options programmes. In spite of such criticism, which is so often justified, it must be asserted that the principles involved in allowing individuals to express a preference are sound. The opportunity to choose is a privilege associated with learning and living, and it would be disturbing if this extremely valuable development in physical education were to be abandoned because of a failure to realise the conditions which must be satisfied and the problems which have to be solved to ensure the successful implementation of a planned, purposeful, progressive programme of work.

General interest and support

Many of the material and human factors which contribute to the development of a successful options programme have been discussed. A further and most important condition which must be satisfied refers to the effect of the options programme on the school as a whole and on the community in general. For real success, support and active cooperation are required, not only from the pupils and the physical education department, but also from the headteacher, other members of staff, school governors, parents and the general public who take an interest in all the activities of the school.

It has already been stated that the headteacher must be so convinced of the value of the scheme that he is willing both to agree to any time-table modifications that might be necessary and to deal sympathetically with any additional financial obligations which the programme may demand. Other members of staff, whose cooperation is essential, should not only be in full agreement with the philosophy and principles involved but should also support fully the methods by which the programme is organised and presented. Only in these circumstances could their complete cooperation be expected and the active participation of those able to make a practical contribution be relied upon whenever required.

Experience has shown that parents have become greatly interested and most impressed by the beneficial effects on their children of this recent development in physical education because of its close link with post-school physical recreation. As a result, their active support is readily available in many ways, such as enthusiastic encouragement of their children to participate; willing provision of suitable dress and items of personal equipment; payment of expenses for travelling to particular sites and centres; personal participation in fund-raising efforts to meet some of the additional expenses which might be incurred in organising and developing this part of the programme.

It is necessary and indeed essential to ensure that the school governors are also fully aware of the nature of the programme being carried out and are in sympathy with all that is being done. Their support, material and otherwise, is invaluable and will make a considerable contribution to ultimate success. Success can often be further enhanced when the fullest possible support is available from others who are in a position to help and whose interest has been stimulated by the many possibilities offered in an options programme. The baths superintendent who is willing to allocate periods for swimming at special times, the parks superintendent who makes arrangements for the provision of games pitches and tennis courts, or the sports centre manager who makes particular facilities available, all are prepared to cooperate, often at some personal inconvenience, because of their firm belief in the many advantages which accrue from this type of programme. The reactions of the general public to what goes on in schools are important and the programme should be seen to be purposeful, sensible and realistic. It is much more satisfying to all concerned if any comments made by members of the public are in favourable and complimentary terms rather than in the form of adverse criticism, much of which is often justified. If such criticism is received, the comments made should lead to essential modifications of the programme with a view to improvement and the hope that the community in general will eventually give full approval and support.

It has been found that members of the general public, even when not closely connected with the school, are very discerning and observant, especially when the school is embarking on new developments which vary from the traditional. The values of well-conducted practical sessions in tennis, ice-skating, fencing, canoeing, golf, and so on are readily appreciated, but it would be more difficult to obtain similar approval for a session in, for example, ten-pin bowling, or indeed in any activity which is either inactive, lacking in continuity and progress, undertaken in facilities which are inadequate, or handicapped by the absence of appropriate tuition. Positive and encouraging comments by the public on any feature of a school's programme constitute a real incentive to further experimentation and development. The options programme in physical education is no exception and many schools have greatly benefitted from the general approval which has been expressed for the successful developments in this field.

The ultimate test of the options programme is the way in which it satisfies the needs and interests of the older pupils. It should be realised however that this final stage of the school's physical education programme is not only the concern of the older pupils and the physical education department of the school, but must be thought of as a project which concerns the entire school staff and everyone connected with the school and its immediate environment. When all these are satisfied there is no doubt of the success achieved, but such success only materialises as a direct result of thorough planning and preparation; efficient organisation; and effective implementation.

Concluding observations on conditions

An endeavour has been made to discuss comprehensively, appropriately and practically the many conditions which should be satisfied in the implementation and development of an options programme in physical education. These conditions can be summarised as follows:

a   suitable facilities;
b   sufficient and appropriate equipment;

c effective coaching;
d a generous staff/pupil ratio;
e groups of a sensible size;
f adequate time allocation;
g a satisfactory range of activities;
h sufficient financial resources;
i maximum participation;
j efficient administration;
k general support.

It might appear that so many exacting conditions have to be satisfied that the organisation of a successful scheme becomes extremely difficult. It cannot be emphasised too much that the organisation of a successful scheme is, in fact, very difficult and it would be true to say that when those concerned in planning an options programme acknowledge that the problems to be faced are considerable, they are already making the first step to real progress. Satisfactory results and a worthwhile end-product are only possible when high standards are set and demanded. If the conditions which have been laid down in this section are satisfied, at least as far as is possible, then success can be confidently expected.

6 How can options be successfully implemented?

Before embarking upon the organisation of a programme of optional activities for older pupils, it is essential to appreciate and understand the principles and problems underlying all that is involved in this comparatively new development in physical education. These aspects have already been dealt with in the preceding sections of this part of the book with the object of providing answers to the following questions:

What is meant by options?
Why introduce optional activities?
When should options be introduced?
What conditions must be satisfied?

A clear understanding of the answers to these questions is necessary to provide a foundation upon which the teacher can assess and evaluate the merits and advantages of an options programme. As a result of such an evaluation he can then decide whether or not to proceed. Sufficient has been said and enough valid reasons have been given to leave no doubt that the introduction of an options programme would be beneficial and popular, but the decision to proceed should

168

be based on a firm conviction that this type of programme is preferable to the more traditional or conventional pattern. Without such a firm conviction it is doubtful whether even the most capable of teachers would be able to implement a programme with complete success. Real enthusiasm is required to overcome the many problems and difficulties which will be met and such enthusiasm can only result from firm conviction. Enthusiasm and conviction are therefore the initial ingredients for success and are the personal qualities required to inspire and indeed to ensure successful planning and preparation.

This leads directly to the question: '*How can an options programme be successfully implemented?*' The first practical point to bear in mind is that a project of this nature should be introduced gradually and with great care. There is nothing to be gained and a lot to be lost by attempting too ambitious a programme before efficient and effective organisation has been established. Too frequently, the mistake is made of changing too drastically from a narrow, conventional, teacher-imposed type of programme to a very liberal options programme which offers too wide a range of alternative activities. In other words, failure and disappointment will often result by changing too quickly from a system which allows no choice at all, to one where too much choice is given. As described in Part Two, Section 6 (see also Fig. 27), four stages were recommended for the development of a school's physical education programme and it will be remembered that the aim in Stage III is to widen and broaden the curriculum in order to provide the necessary experience upon which the pupils can make a sensible choice in Stage IV (the options stage). When the teacher and the physical education department as a whole are satisfied with the results achieved in Stage III, they can more confidently proceed to a system which allows individuals to express a preference.

If a decision has been made that an options programme is to be introduced, it must be assumed:

a   that the problems involved have been realised and the conditions which should be satisfied – e.g. facilities, equipment, staffing, coaching, administration, etc. – carefully considered;

b   that all those directly involved in conducting the scheme have expressed their willingness to cooperate.

Directing the options programme

Since efficient administration and thorough organisation are vital to success, it will be readily appreciated that one person must have the ultimate responsibility for the detailed directing of the programme.

169

This duty is normally undertaken by the head of the physical education department. Where the senior man and woman specialists enjoy equal status in the school, these administrative duties would be their joint concern unless an arrangement has been made for one or other to accept this as a personal responsibility. This latter policy has advantages, especially when decisions have to be made, sometimes at short notice, on controversial issues or conflicting demands such as the allocation of facilities to particular groups, the deployment of staff, the availability of equipment, and so on. Even so, the person in charge is well advised to have frequent consultations with all colleagues who are involved in the scheme and to discuss thoroughly with all who might be personally concerned those matters on which decisions have to be made which affect day-to-day organisation. Cooperation and collaboration are important factors in ensuring the successful operation of the options programme.

Implementing the scheme and the use of pro formae

Bearing in mind the many factors which have to be considered, the range of activities to be offered must then be determined. It is recommended that, initially, the activities available should be limited in number and that the introductory phase of the scheme should be regarded as largely experimental until everything appears to be working smoothly and to the satisfaction of both pupils and staff.

It is wise, even though a limited number of activities might be offered, to make as much use as possible of the services of those members of staff who are to participate in the full scheme. This will ensure the maintenance of their interest and enable them to be involved personally in the initial phase of the project. It will also permit the additional advantage of operating with small groups of pupils, thus increasing the staff–pupil ratio.

Having decided upon the actual activities which are to be made available, the next step is to ascertain the preferences of the pupils themselves. This information must be obtained well in advance so that all the necessary preparations can be completed in good time and to allow the staff opportunities to resolve any problems or difficulties. For this purpose a pro forma will be required for each pupil involved in the scheme. The pro forma must show the available activities from which a choice must be made, with space for the pupil to indicate at least three chosen activities in order of priority. A suggested type of pro forma for this purpose is shown in Fig. 39 on page 171. A completed pro forma is shown in Fig. 40 on page 172. This pro forma is based on the requirements for one term only and deliberately in-

PHYSICAL EDUCATION
The Options Programme

NAME...................... FORM ....

TERM .... YEAR..........................

AVAILABLE ACTIVITIES

1st choice

2nd choice

3rd choice

4th choice

Signature   ....

FIGURE 39   *The options programme – a suitable pro forma*

cludes a limited choice of available alternatives to emphasise the firm belief that a limited choice is the best and most successful way of introducing the scheme. Later, influenced by the success enjoyed in the earlier stages, it might be possible to expand the range of aspects offered, as illustrated in Fig. 41 on page 173, but this part of the administration remains essentially the same.

When the pro formae have been completed, the preferences expressed by the pupils must be analysed and the pupils allocated to appropriate groups in accordance with the predetermined plan or pattern. In other words, if the available activities are soccer, rugby, basketball and swimming, the director will know in advance how many pupils can be accommodated in each group. Though this allocation to groups and activities is not always straightforward, the aim should be to enable each pupil to participate in the activity of his

PHYSICAL EDUCATION
The Options Programme

NAME...G.F.Smith............ FORM...IV A...............

TERM ..Autumn............ YEAR....1971-2..............

AVAILABLE ACTIVITIES

Association Football   Rugby Football

Basketball   Swimming

1st choice   *Swimming*

2nd choice   *Basketball*

3rd choice   *Association Football*

4th choice

Signature .... *Gordon J. Smith*......

FIGURE 40   *The options programme – example of completed pro forma*

first choice. When this is not possible, second and sometimes third choices must be brought into consideration and careful records should be kept to ensure that first choice activities can be allocated later.

An important feature of the organisation at this stage is to ensure that everyone concerned is made fully aware of the detailed information which they require. At least three copies of the details of the allocation of pupils to groups will be needed – one for the director which will be kept as an official record, one for the member of staff in charge of the group and one for the notice-board for the information of the pupils. To include too much detail on these lists can lead to confusion but certain essential facts will be necessary, such as:

a   the duration of the activity (e.g. term and year);

b   the activity (e.g. basketball);

172

PHYSICAL EDUCATION
The Options Programme

NAME ..W.K.Jordan.......... FORM ...VI.B..............

TERM ..Summer.............. YEAR....1971-2...........

AVAILABLE ACTIVITIES

Athletics   Swimming
Badminton   Tennis
Cricket   Volleyball
Golf   Sailing

1st choice   *Golf*

2nd choice   *Athletics*

3rd choice   *Tennis*

4th choice   *Sailing*

Signature   *William H. Jordan*

FIGURE 41   *The options programme – another example*

c   the venue (e.g. gymnasium);
d   the time and day (e.g. 2.30 p.m. to 4.00 p.m. Wednesdays);
e   the name of the teacher in charge;
f   the names of the pupils in the group.

Ideally, it is an advantage if this information is available and circulated before the end of the term preceding the one in which the activities will operate, so that all the necessary preparations can be completed for starting immediately at the beginning of the new term. Careful preliminary planning and preparation such as this is one of the most important factors of a successful options programme, ensuring as it does that all concerned, pupils and staff, know exactly what is happening and what is expected of them. Unfortunately, success is frequently prevented because of the confusion caused by inadequate preparation and communication.

It is necessary to repeat this procedure each term and then to record the details of the activities pursued by each pupil. The principle behind an options programme is that the needs of each individual pupil are being catered for and therefore the recording of the programme followed by each pupil in any given year is an essential aspect of the administration, even though this may appear to be a somewhat laborious task. For this purpose, a second pro forma is recommended which would enable this vital recording to be done as simply and yet as concisely as possible. The pro forma must clearly indicate the activities pursued by the individual during each term of the year or years in which he participates in the options programme. A suitable pro forma for this purpose is illustrated in Fig. 42 (page 176). It will be seen that this pro forma is applicable to an options programme which extends over a period of two years, but if necessary it could easily be modified for recording a programme of longer duration. This type of pro forma is useful for a number of reasons. For example:

a   it records the activities pursued by each pupil in each term;

b   if completed regularly, it serves as a guide for the allocation of a pupil to his new activity in each term and in the second or subsequent years of the scheme. This will be done in accordance with the agreed policy of the school. (See Section 5, page 159 – How many activities for each pupil?);

c   completed pro formae will show the activities which are popular or otherwise and when analysed will indicate whether modifications to the range of activities available or in the facilities provided should be considered;

d   if the policy of the school permits pupils to participate in an activity for a second time in the second or subsequent years of the scheme, the completed pro formae will show not only the particular interests of individual pupils but also which activities, because of their popularity, are chosen for a second time.

The reasons for the popularity of particular activities are of great interest and often reflect the success and achievement of the pupils, the standard of the facilities available and the calibre of the organisation and instruction.

Figure 43 (page 176) illustrates a completed pro forma for a two-year programme. If, for any reason, such as limited facilities or insufficient staff, it is necessary to restrict participation in particular activities to a shorter period, in order to accommodate the pupils' requirements, this information, as indicated, can be recorded satisfactorily on the same pro forma.

Since the information provided is a permanent record of each pupil's activities, the completed pro forma should be readily accessible for reference purposes. For this reason, it is recommended that if the scheme operates for more than one year, the pro forma should be completed on a year rather than a form or class basis, with the pupils' names in alphabetical order. In the case of mixed schools, when some of the groups might operate as mixed groups, it may be advantageous to record the activities of boys and girls separately, but the suggested pro forma caters for either arrangement.

To ensure effective administration of the programme, copies of the pro formae, as illustrated in Figs 39 and 42, should always be readily available. Provision would normally be the responsibility of the school, but where options programmes are well established in an authority, the pro formae might well be issued in bulk to the schools concerned by the education office.

The administrative arrangements which have been suggested, and which are considered essential for success, apply particularly to an options programme which operates in sessions of at least double-period duration. It has been suggested earlier that single-period options can also be successfully implemented, but since these are normally conducted on a class basis, with only one teacher in charge of each class, the organisation required is much more the individual teacher's own responsibility. The basic factors related to facilities, equipment, supervision, continuity, range of available activities, preferences of pupils, allocation to groups, recording, etc., apply equally to single-period options and the use of the pro formae suggested in Figs 39 and 42, even though some modifications might be necessary, would still prove to be equally valuable.

Staffing and mixed groups

When organising an options programme, it is recommended that the teacher in charge of any group should be the most suitable person for that particular activity, whatever the sex of the teacher or pupils. In other words, there is no reason why, for example, a boys' group in swimming should not be taken by a woman, or a girls' group in athletics by a man. If this principle is accepted, not only is the organisation of the programme simplified, but it often becomes possible to offer a wider range of activities. At all times, the aim should be to exploit to the full the talents of the staff, in order to cater for the activities chosen by the pupils and although the view is sometimes expressed that boys should be taken by men and girls by women, it is felt that many activities in the options programme need not come into these categories.

PHYSICAL EDUCATION
The Options Programme

Individual Records

NAME	YEAR	AUTUMN	SPRING	SUMMER

FIGURE 42 *The options programme – individual records*

PHYSICAL EDUCATION
The Options Programme

Individual Records

NAME	YEAR	AUTUMN	SPRING	SUMMER
W.J.Anderson	1970-1	Soccer	X.C.R./Gym.	Athletics
	1971-2	Basketball	Soccer	Athletics
M.C.Brown	1970-1	Rugby	Gym./Judo	Swimming
	1971-2	Rugby	Basketball	Cricket
A.F.Chambers	1970-1	Trampolining	Swimming	Sailing
	1971-2	Gymnastics	Fenc'g/Swim.	Golf
E.H.Davidson	1970-1	Badminton	Swimming	Tennis
	1971-2	Fencing	Swim./Bad'n	Volleyball

FIGURE 43 *The options programme – a method of recording*

A further issue to be resolved in implementing the options programme is the question of mixed groups. It is obvious that some activities will, of necessity, be single-sex activities (e.g. cricket, rugby, rounders, or netball), but many of the other aspects can be successfully organised in mixed groups, often with distinct advantages. Badminton, tennis, fencing, archery and volleyball are some examples of activities in which both sexes can participate together and sometimes compete against each other without detriment to the enjoyment factor or the development of better standards. There are also distinct social values to be gained from joint participation and this creates a situation which is much more closely related to that which prevails in adult clubs. Many activities, such as swimming, sailing, athletics, rock-climbing and canoeing, have often flourished much more successfully with older pupils when organised as mixed rather than single-sex groups. In addition, there is an administrative and practical advantage to be gained from the inclusion of mixed groups in the scheme. A wider range of activities becomes possible when boys and girls can be combined into one group, especially if otherwise there might not be a sufficient number of either sex to form a group of worthwhile size. For example, eight boys and eight girls together would constitute a satisfactory number for a fencing group which, if conducted as two separate groups, might prove uneconomical from the staffing point of view. By combining pupils in this way, the possibility of eliminating the activity from the range of those available can often be avoided.

It is appreciated that opinions often differ on the question of mixed or single-sex groups and of men taking girls or women taking boys. If this issue becomes a problem, consultation amongst the staff should take place in order that an agreed decision can be reached. Consultation with the pupils themselves is also extremely valuable, for their views at this stage can often be a most effective and reliable guide.

School clubs

In Part Two, Section 7 (page 116), the contribution which school clubs can make to the physical education programme as a whole was thoroughly discussed. Clubs flourish because the pupils participate in activities of their own choice and in which they have ability and interest. Optional activities are in many ways a development and an extension of the principles which initially prompted the formation of school clubs, the essential difference being that options are normally conducted during school hours. School clubs can very effectively supplement the options programme:

a   by providing additional opportunities for further participation and tuition for those pupils who desire to make even more progress than is possible during school hours;

b   by providing opportunity for participation in a particular activity which, for many reasons, it may not be possible to include as one of the options offered.

177

Concluding observations on implementation

Whilst material factors such as facilities, equipment, staffing, and so on play an important part, the key to real success in the implementation of an options programme is the attention which must be given to careful planning, thorough preparation, effective organisation and efficient administration. These are vital factors which have a great influence on all those involved in the scheme. Without them, chaos, frustration and disappointment inevitably result and the standards reached give no sense of satisfaction either to staff or pupils.

In the presentation of any aspect of a physical education programme, no less than in the presentation of any lesson, academic or practical, teaching begins where organisation ends. Because of the complexity of the situation this is particularly true of an options programme in physical education, but when effective organisation, assisted by the use of the recommended pro formae, is supplemented by expert tuition, chaos, frustration and disappointment are replaced by satisfaction, enjoyment and the attainment of worth-while standards.

7 Where must a line be drawn?

This is probably the most important question of all. The problems related to an options programme must be viewed with commonsense and balanced judgement and must be approached with a clear realisation of the many conditions which must be satisfied. This stage of the programme must be put into the right perspective in relation to the requirements of the physical education programme as a whole, and discretion must be exercised in the introduction and presentation of the new ideas involved. This final stage, which allows individuals to select activities in which they have special interest and ability, is sound in principle and popular in practice, but it should never be allowed to become a travesty of physical education, inviting and deserving the adverse criticisms it sometimes receives. Options should never become an easy way out of involvement in worthwhile physical activity. Personal selection should lead to more purposeful, enjoyable, sustained and profitable participation than the traditional type of programme made possible.

Reference to Section 5 ('What conditions must be satisfied?') will lead to the answers to the question 'Where should a line be drawn?' If:

a   an activity is not appropriate for inclusion in a physical education programme;
b   an activity is not physically demanding;
c   facilities are substandard;
d   equipment is in short supply;
e   efficient coaching is not available;
f   the staff–pupil ratio is inadequate;
g   a satisfactory time allocation cannot be guaranteed;
h   financial resources are not sufficient;
i   administrative requirements cannot be met;
j   general support is not obtained;
k   the overall physical education programme of the school suffers adversely, because of demands made by the options programme,
then a line must be drawn and the common sense and balanced judgement already referred to must be applied in order that the scheme can be introduced, if necessary modified, and developed with maximum success.

If this stage of the programme is presented with care and thought it should contribute to the well-being of pupils – physically, educationally, recreationally and socially – and should help to solve many of the problems of the 'leisure explosion' in post-school years.

8 Final comments

'Generations of educators have deplored the rigidity of classroom settings and curriculum content that force pupils into a common mould.' Recent developments in the teaching of physical education have been based on the needs of individuals and with the specific aim of satisfying the principles and philosophy which are implied in this quotation. The introduction of a scheme of optional activities for older pupils is a further development of this philosophy, but how is this philosophy interpreted in practice? It would appear that there are three basic interpretations:

a   Activities are made available only when *facilities and equipment* are adequate. This provides maximum participation and can be identified as *recreation*.
b   Activities are made available when *facilities and equipment* exist as in (*a*) above, but only when adequate *supervision* can also be provided, especially in those aspects where safety and supervision are of special significance. This situation could be defined as *controlled recreation*.

c Only those activities are made available where –

i) *facilities and equipment* allow for active participation;

ii) *adequate supervision* is provided;

iii) *instruction* and *coaching* are available.

These combine to produce a learning situation and since the activities are individually selected by the pupils, this could be described as a *recreative learning situation*.

The three interpretations therefore seem to be:

a participation only;

b participation with supervision;

c participation with supervision and tuition.

Can all three alternatives justify a place in the programme? Can they be complementary to each other? Can they exist side by side? It is believed that the answer to these questions is yes, even though it would be hoped that every situation in the options programme would, whenever possible, approach the standards envisaged in (*c*) above. Responsible pupils should, at times, be expected to control and conduct their own recreation – this is surely a desirable end-product of a successful physical education programme. Selected pupils, whose sense of responsibility is beyond question, could sometimes be invited to assist with supervision and occasionally with tuition, thus helping with the problem of providing a satisfactory staff–pupil ratio and giving the pupils a sense of involvement and satisfaction. Of the three methods of presenting options, the third must be regarded as the most desirable, but there could be a valuable, even though supplementary, contribution made by the other two.

Sufficient has been said to indicate that a scheme of optional activities for older pupils is considered to be an essential feature of a successful physical education curriculum. Moreover, this way of presenting the final stage of the programme will become even more important as more and more pupils stay longer at school. Beyond doubt, this is an exciting and worthwhile development in physical education and should be given every consideration and encouragement. Though it is acknowledged that the problems of implementation are many, they are not insuperable and the rewards give great satisfaction to both pupils and teachers.

It is hoped that the recommendations which have been made and the guidance which has been given will be of help and value to all those who are involved in the physical education of older pupils and will inspire and stimulate the introduction and development of many successful options programmes.

Part Four

Conclusions

1 A general review

In recent years, the expanding curriculum in physical education, together with the considerable developments which have taken place in the teaching methods employed in its presentation, have combined to make the work of the specialist teacher more difficult and complex. New ideas, new methods and techniques – necessary aspects of a developing society or a progressive education – have a refreshing influence upon accepted theory and practice, so it is essential that teachers should be progressive in outlook and attitude. It is equally important that they should understand the principles underlying their work and what they hope to achieve, especially when new ideas are being explored and introduced. Experience in the last few years, however, has shown that care and discretion should be exercised to ensure that over-concentration on the more theoretical aspects of physical education does not lead to neglect of the very real, practical problems of presentation and implementation.

There is little doubt that the indoctrination of both students and teachers with new ideas and philosophies has been almost an obsession with many of those who have been directly concerned with the initial or further training of teachers. This has led, in many instances, to a reduction and diminution of emphasis on the practical problems of teaching, with the result that many teachers, especially the young and inexperienced, have found it difficult to plan and prepare their curriculum and to organise, introduce and develop their programmes of work satisfactorily. However sound the theories and philosophies, however clearly they are understood, the time comes when the teacher is face to face with the realistic, practical, day-to-day problems of teaching. Unfortunately, for one reason or another, many teachers seem unable to face this situation confidently and with any measure of security. Specific guidance is required, not only in the content of their programmes and the methods used in the implementation of the many aspects now undertaken, but also in the organisation of their curriculum and in the actual techniques of teaching.

In Part One of this book, an attempt was made to describe the many changes which have affected the development of physical education during the last two or more decades, to evaluate these developments and to assess their impact on the content of the curriculum and the teaching methods used. It is important that all those involved in the administrative, as well as the professional aspects of teaching, should be familiar with these changes and should clearly understand their implications in order that their own work can be effectively related to past experience and current thought. The whole field of education and the many changes which have taken place in recent years are the concern of all teachers, including subject specialists. Equally, it is important that all involved in education should be aware of and interested in the developments which have taken place in physical education, even though they themselves may not be directly concerned. 'A teacher, primary or secondary, is at all times concerned with children. He attempts to educate them through the medium of a specific subject – hence it is the end product of the educated child that is of importance, not the child's particular skill in a single aspect of education.' The ultimate goals of education and physical education are therefore inseparable. 'Educational development is a total process, so the ultimate aim of physical education coincides with the general objective of all education – to develop healthy responsible citizens capable of assuming their place in society.'

The trends and developments referred to in Part One, especially the expansion in the scope and content of the subject and the changes in teaching method, have made the successful planning of a physical education programme much more complex and demanding. This formidable task requires to be undertaken in a much more thoughtful and systematic way than was previously required and in Part Two an endeavour has been made to show how this can be done. The philosophies and principles upon which a successful curriculum is based have been discussed, but the primary aim has been to give help and guidance in solving realistically the many problems which have to be faced when planning an effective and balanced programme. It is appreciated that planning a programme is an individual matter, but the need for detailed evaluation and thorough preparation cannot be over-emphasised. These important aspects of teaching must be given careful consideration, otherwise the programme will have serious limitations and its implementation will be inferior and unsatisfactory.

The modern conception of physical education implies a comprehensive programme, in which the final stage presents to the individual pupil opportunities to choose from a number of available alternatives. The particular problems which require careful consideration when implementing such a programme have been discussed in Part Three. It has been said that 'making pupils, especially older pupils, do what they don't like doing, is the first step in encouraging them to drop that pursuit at the earliest possible opportunity'. There is some validity in this statement and so the options programme is a welcome and valuable innovation. But it has also been said, with equal justification, that 'compulsion and choice should be in the right degree, for too much of one is as bad as too little of the other'. Freedom is greatly valued and desired, but 'freedom should be compatible with order, because all freedom perishes under disorder'. It is on such ideas and principles as these that the suggestions made for a developing physical education programme are based, a programme which begins with a basic course of a limited number of teacher-selected activities, progressing gradually to a wider curriculum and leading ultimately to a final stage where individual choice is permitted.

Emphasis has been given to the teacher's responsibilities for ensuring that opportunities are provided throughout the whole of the physical education programme for pupils to develop powers of sensible discrimination. Of Sir Winston Churchill, the Duke of Edinburgh once said, 'He had the gift of real discrimination, which is so much more valuable than the automatic acceptance of anything new and the facile rejection of anything old.' If the aim of education is to help children to grow to the full, then they must also grow in their capacity to discriminate and to make responsible decisions for themselves.

2   The involvement of physical education staff

It cannot be denied that if the physical education curriculum in schools is viewed in the light of the many facets which have been discussed, the demands made upon the P.E. specialist are extremely exacting. The personal qualities and the technical ability demanded of teachers during actual lessons are themselves formidable, especially when the problem of safety is added to the need to maintain interest, to stimulate physical effort and to ensure progress. But when careful planning and efficient organisation of a very wide curriculum become an additional challenge, the magnitude of the teacher's task can be readily appreciated.

To undertake such a task satisfactorily requires marked ability –

physical and intellectual – and also a willingness to make the necessary mental and physical efforts to ensure success. The successful P.E. teacher must therefore have an inspiring personality, conviction in the methods he uses, knowledge of his subject, skill in implementation, a conscientious attitude towards preparation, and the ability and determination to demand and obtain high standards. In other words, for real success, physical education, no less than any other subject in the curriculum, requires teachers of the highest calibre.

Having said this, it is perhaps appropriate to acknowledge the very valuable contribution made by teachers in the wider realms of physical education, sport and recreation, frequently beyond the boundaries of their own school. The extent to which many teachers become involved in out-of-school and inter-school activities and competitions is considerable. Such involvement, together with the demands of the normal school programme, is summarised in Fig. 44 on page 186 to emphasise the comprehensive nature and the indisputable challenge of physical education today.

3 A formula for success

The intention in this book has been to discuss the complex nature of the physical education curriculum, but even more to give practical help and guidance in solving satisfactorily the problems of implementation. It is felt therefore that it will be helpful to conclude by giving a concise summary of those factors or ingredients which constitute a formula for success. These are:

a Evaluation

The teacher must study, evaluate and assess the many factors, material and human, which influence the planning of the physical education curriculum as a whole, the planning of the scheme of work for each aspect of the programme and the preparation of each lesson within each aspect.

b Preparation

Following evaluation, the teacher is then in a position to plan his overall programme and schemes of work and to prepare adequately and thoroughly the detailed requirements of his lessons. It is essential that the selection of material and the methods to be used must be

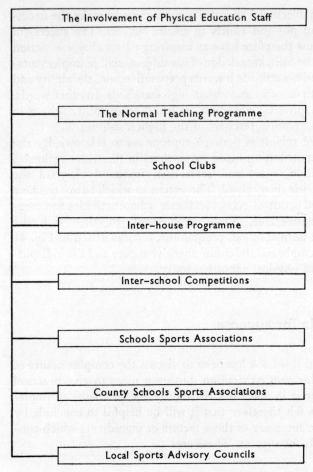

```
┌─────────────────────────────────────────────────┐
│   The Involvement of Physical Education Staff     │
└─────────────────────────────────────────────────┘
        ┌───────────────────────────────────┐
        │     The Normal Teaching Programme  │
        └───────────────────────────────────┘
        ┌───────────────────────────────────┐
        │             School Clubs           │
        └───────────────────────────────────┘
        ┌───────────────────────────────────┐
        │        Inter-house Programme       │
        └───────────────────────────────────┘
        ┌───────────────────────────────────┐
        │       Inter-school Competitions    │
        └───────────────────────────────────┘
        ┌───────────────────────────────────┐
        │      Schools Sports Associations   │
        └───────────────────────────────────┘
        ┌───────────────────────────────────┐
        │  County Schools Sports Associations│
        └───────────────────────────────────┘
        ┌───────────────────────────────────┐
        │     Local Sports Advisory Councils │
        └───────────────────────────────────┘
```

FIGURE 44   *The involvement of physical education staff*

appropriate to the situation which has been established as a result of the information obtained and the decisions made during evaluation.

c   Time allocation

In order to obtain worthwhile standards in any aspect of physical education, a sufficient allocation of time must be given to provide ample opportunity for repetition, revision and recapitulation; concentration, consolidation and continuity.

d   Teacher inspiration and stimulation

'Teachers must teach' and this involves making the fullest use of the basic techniques of good teaching, both verbal and visual. 'Telling, coaching, guiding, imposing, challenging and demanding are fundamental in any teaching situation and must be acceptable in the presentation of physical education.'

e   Perfection

A constant demand for high standards is essential, but this must be related to the individual pupil's potential ability and capacity, rather than to a uniform class or group standard. Pupils give what is demanded of them and if little is demanded, little will be given. Teachers should expect the best that each pupil can give for there is little doubt that positive expectations bring positive results.

One of the most effective motivating influences in the production of worthwhile standards is the individual's realisation that progress has been made. Teachers should ensure that each pupil experiences, as frequently as possible, a sense of achievement. In every teaching situation the value of praise should never be underestimated but, 'praise, like gold and silver, owes its value to its sincerity' (Samuel Johnson).

The formula for success therefore, is:

evaluation of the influencing factors;
appropriate preparation;
time for repetition and consolidation;
teacher inspiration and stimulation;
demands for *individual perfection*.

When all these ingredients are present, the formula is complete and the end-product will be successful and satisfactory work. On the other hand, if one or other of the component parts is absent, the formula is incomplete and the standard of work is greatly diminished.

Recent developments in physical education have emerged from the realisation that each pupil is an individual, with individual characteristics related to physique, physical ability, aptitude and attitude. Of equal significance is the individuality of each teacher whose personality is often reflected in his philosophy and the methods he adopts. Moreover, the successful development of physical education lies in the ability of each teacher to experiment courageously, to clarify his principles, to keep a balanced view on what he hopes to achieve, and to select the material and methods of presentation which will best meet these ends.

It is hoped that the information and guidance given in this book will stimulate new ideas, inspire experimentation, and give help and encouragement to all those engaged in developing patterns in physical education.

Index

Page numbers in italics indicate illustrative material